Coping with England

To Peter, who is my reason for living in this beautiful and fascinating country, and to Mom, who has to cope with my being so far away

"This is Waterloo, Sir — I think you want Euston..."

Coping with England

Jean Hannah

Basil Blackwell

Copyright © Jean Hannah 1987

First published 1987

Basil Blackwell Ltd
108 Cowley Road, Oxford OX4 1JF, UK

Basil Blackwell Inc.
432 Park Avenue South, Suite 1503,
New York, NY 10016, USA

British Library Cataloguing in Publication Data

Hannah, Jean
   Coping with England.
   1. England – Description and travel –
   1971– – Guide-books
   I. Title
   914.2′04858   DA650

   ISBN 0-631-13557-X
   ISBN 0-631-13726-2 Pbk

Library of Congress Cataloging in Publication Data

Hannah, Jean.
   Coping with England.

   Includes index.
   1. Great Britain – Description and travel – 1971-
   2. Great Britain – Social life and customs – 20 century.
   3. National characteristics, British. I. Title.
   DA632.H345   1987   941.085   86-13666
   ISBN 0-631-13557-X
   ISBN 0-631-13726-2 Pbk

Typeset by Opus, Oxford
Printed in Great Britain by Billing and Sons Ltd, Worcester

Contents

Acknowledgments

I would like to thank those people who have taken the time to give me comments and advice on the typescript of this book. They include: Harriet Barry, Colin Biggs, Christel Butcher, Sue Chambers, John Davey, Alice Davison, Rosemary Hannah, Lauren Johnson, Kim Lewis, Maria Sifianou, Sue Thacker, Peter Trudgill, Keith Walters, and Ray Ward. Many other people, too numerous to cite here, have helped by raising or discussing specific points that have made their way into the contents. Finally, this book would never have been written without the constant encouragement, moral support, and patience of my husband, Peter Trudgill.

Introduction

This is not a normal guidebook to England. It does not tell you where to go, what to see, or where to stay. Instead, it offers helpful information about what to expect, what to say, how to behave, and how to do things in various situations – in other words, how to cope with being in a foreign country.

The amount of difficulty you will have in coping with England will depend to a large degree on where you come from and how long you stay. While this book is aimed at English-speaking visitors and has, admittedly, an American bias (which I can't help, since I am an American), I have also tried to discuss aspects of the English way of life that Europeans and other foreigners might find particularly strange. I've included information that should be relevant to a variety of visitors to these shores – short-term 'holiday-makers,' businesspeople, and those intending to stay for a longer period of time. Where I've used British terms, the U.S. equivalents appear afterwards in parentheses.

As the title suggests, this book focuses on England, although some of my remarks hold for the rest of Britain as well. I have occasionally included information specific to Scotland and Wales; but please do not take these fleeting comments as representing the only differences between the English and Celtic ways of doing things – even the English need a guidebook to the finer details of coping in these 'foreign' lands! Such advice will, I hope, find its way into other books in the 'Coping with . . .' series.

A book of this nature cannot be entirely objective. I have drawn generalizations from my own observations, and the things that I may have found bemusing or amusing in England are not necessarily the same as those that other foreigners will notice. So if you find that there are details that I have left out, not discussed enough, or just gotten wrong, please fill out the Suggestions page at the end of the book and send it in.

Although I have included some criticisms of England and the English, I hope that it will be clear to you (and to all my English friends) that I genuinely like this country and its inhabitants. I feel fortunate to live in such a beautiful, interesting, and cultured place. And my stay here has been made all the more enjoyable because of the truly nice English people – my husband, in-laws, friends, and acquaintances – who have laughed with me (and sometimes at me) as they have tried to help me understand and cope with living in England.

Going there

England offers plenty of interesting things to do and see whatever time of the year you decide to go there. If you are lucky enough to have some choice over when you travel, there are several factors that may influence your decision, depending upon what you want to see and do. Some places and types of entertainment are open or available only at certain times of the year. For example, during the winter many seaside hotels and historic homes are closed; and several of the top theater, opera, and ballet companies tour at various times. Or you may be worried about the infamous British weather affecting your plans (see Climate, p. 4), or wish to avoid crowds of other tourists and get cheaper hotel rates during the off season.

When to go

The main tourist season runs from Easter to mid-October, with the heaviest influx of visitors being from June through August. Most English people take their holidays between the end of July and the end of August, so it is more difficult at those times to find accommodation as well as peace and quiet. If you are traveling during the height of the season, be sure to make advance bookings (reservations) for lodgings and buy tickets for special events in advance too, if possible.

Tourist season

Legal holidays, when the banks and most shops are closed and the natives are on the loose, are:

Holidays

New Year's Day (January 1); also January 2 in
   Scotland
Good Friday and Easter Monday (dates vary);
   only Good Friday in Scotland
May Day (first Monday in May); not observed
   in Scotland

May Bank Holiday (public holiday) (last Monday
   in May)
August Bank Holiday (last Monday in August in
   England and Wales; first Monday in August in
   Scotland)
Christmas Day and Boxing Day (December 25
   and 26)

In addition, there are school half-term holidays,
usually lasting a week, at the end of October,
February, and May, as well as two- or three-week
school breaks at Christmas and Easter. During these
times, trains are filled with families going off to visit
relatives, and the cities and popular spots are crowded
with children.

Climate   The English climate has a bad reputation, which is
only partially deserved. Many foreigners think that
the country (especially London) is perpetually
shrouded in fog or coated with drizzle. This, of
course, is not true. Many of the fog problems of the
past were actually due to smog and have cleared up
with pollution controls. And even though the natives
usually carry umbrellas, this doesn't mean that it is
always raining – just that it *might* rain.

Although England is quite far north (London is at
almost the same latitude as Calgary, Canada), it is
warmed by the Gulf Stream and 'enjoys' a maritime
climate. This means that the weather is mild, wet, and
changeable. The English think that their weather is
quite civilized: they don't suffer from extremes of
temperature or from tornadoes, typhoons, prolonged
droughts, or floods. What they do suffer from is
dampness. Frequent but light rains keep the grass a
lovely fresh green all year round, but in the winter
and on cool days the high humidity can chill you to
the bone. England also suffers from constant weather
records – the wettest March, the sunniest Easter, the
coldest August, etc.

In fact, the only thing that can be said about the
weather with any certainty is that it is highly
changeable. Perhaps that is why the inhabitants are
always commenting on it. Don't be fooled by a clear,
sunny sky; clouds and rain can move in quickly. On

the other hand, what may look like a dull, overcast day can turn into a beautiful warm and sunny one. There are few cloudless days, but you can usually glimpse the sun. at some point. And the changing cloud formations at least have the advantage of providing interesting backgrounds for photographs.

Because of the fickleness of the climate, weather reports are devised to be evasive. Most forecasts are prefaced by 'probably,' 'possibly' or 'it looks as if it might,' so that you're never exactly sure what to expect. You have to be a master of subtleties to figure out the differences among some of the more common weather jargon, such as: 'partly sunny,' 'partly cloudy,' 'some sunshine,' 'intermittent sunshine,' 'sunny spells,' 'sunny intervals,' 'sunny periods,' 'sun breaking through from time to time,' 'partly cloudy,' 'cloudy patches,' and 'bright' (which doesn't exclude clouds or rain); or 'some rain,' 'rain at times,' 'outbreaks of rain,' 'showers,' 'showery weather with bright intervals,' and 'stormy weather.' Whatever the weather reports say, be prepared for just about anything; always take an umbrella with you, and a jacket or sweater too.

Since the weather is so variable, it is dangerous to generalize about the seasons, but the following may be taken as a rough guide.

Seasons

Summer runs from June through early September. Temperatures are usually pleasantly warm during the day (in the south, the 70s F / 20s C), and there can be a lot of sunshine. The humidity tends to be lower than at other times of the year, meaning there are few very sticky days. But the nights can be cool occasionally, and if you are unlucky you may even need to put the heating on. If there is a prolonged heat spell (that is, a few days over 80°F), it makes the headlines of the newspapers, people complain about it, and everyone suffers when indoors because few people have air conditioners or even fans. June and September tend to have drier and more stable weather than the other summer months.

Summer

In the south, the sea is usually warm enough to swim in all summer long, but elsewhere it may not warm up enough for most people's comfort until July. The Gulf Stream warms the entire west coast, though, so swimming can be enjoyed all the way up to the northwest coast of Scotland.

Since Britain lies so far north in the world, it stays light quite late in the summer – until about 9:30 p.m. in the south and 10:30 p.m. in Scotland. It also gets light much earlier in the morning than you may expect – it isn't uncommon to be woken at 4:30 or 5 a.m. by birds singing merrily.

Autumn   Autumn (not 'fall') lasts from late September to late November. Near the end of September, dampness sets in, especially in the north. The weather everywhere can be heavily overcast and drizzly for days on end, although there are also cool, dry, and sunny spells. Autumn is fog season for some areas, with the mist descending late at night and sometimes not lifting until late morning. Nights and mornings are usually quite cool.

The autumnal colors are pretty rather than spectacular, with most leaves turning various shades of yellow. In moorlands in early autumn, carpets of beautiful purple heather color the countryside.

Winter   Late November through February can be a cold, damp, gray period, with January being particularly awful. However, bright sunny spells sometimes break the gloom of the short days (the sun sets near 4 p.m.). Night frosts are common away from the coast, but temperatures almost always climb above freezing during the day. Freezing fog is a special (and dreadful) weather condition that can descend at night and in the early morning hours, providing the dual problem of thick fog and icy road surfaces. Light hail or sleet is also fairly common.

The south rarely gets more than a trace of snow, except in the hills, and any snow that does accumulate usually doesn't last long. As in many other places with mild climates, if more than a few inches of snow falls, daily life grinds to a halt. The English just don't know how to cope with snow, and hardly anyone owns a snow shovel. Many people don't even own a winter hat or thick gloves, pretending cold weather doesn't exist by not preparing for it. In hilly and exposed areas of England, Scotland, and Wales, snow falls more often and stays longer, sometimes blocking roads.

Spring runs from March through May. Early spring can be quite wet, but the burst of flowers, the blossoming trees and shrubs, and the amazing variety of shades of green compensate for overcast days. May is often the time to see England at its best (especially the famous gardens). Temperatures are generally mild during the day, but overnight frosts can continue into May. Periods of warm weather come and go.

Spring

The far southwest tends to be the warmest region of England, although it is also often wetter than other areas. You may even be able to walk around in a short-sleeved shirt on the occasional winter day. The area has few frosts, and spring comes very early.

Regional differences

The Midlands are colder during the winter than the coastal areas, while the north is usually colder and damper in general than other regions. East Anglia is the driest region, but it often suffers from cold winds off the North Sea.

The Lake District is far wetter than most other regions, with approximately two hundred rainy days a year. (See pp. 49–50 for the location of regions.)

Most people, tourists and business travelers alike, will encounter little red tape in being admitted to England. Citizens of countries in the EEC (European Economic Community, also called the EC and the Common Market) need only proof of nationality, while citizens of most other countries need only a valid passport. A recent change is that citizens of India, Pakistan, Bangladesh, Ghana, and Nigeria must get a visa before coming to Britain. Most tourists are automatically granted a six-month stay.

Red tape
Visas

If you want to stay in England for a longer period (to study or work, for example), you need a visa and have to show that you have enough money to support yourself during that time. Work permits for most jobs are difficult to get: you need to have professional qualifications or a high degree of skill or experience and must prove that no one in Britain or the EC can fill the position. You do not need a work permit, however, if you can prove that one of your grandparents or parents was born in Britain. Note that a student visa or work permit does not give you the right to residency after your course or job is finished. Long-stay visa holders must register with the local police on arrival (except for some Commonwealth citizens).

Immigration   Immigrating to England is an increasingly difficult matter. Because England is a small country with a large population, a strained welfare system, and growing unemployment, and because of an increase in the number of immigrants from different cultural backgrounds, there has been much pressure to reduce the number of people allowed to settle in the country. The present government has tightened immigration controls substantially and has taken away the right of automatic residency from most former colonial citizens. Women who have residency in Britain but who aren't British nationals cannot automatically bring foreign husbands into the country (although this is being challenged in the courts).

An immigrant can become a naturalized citizen after five years of living in Britain if he or she can show sufficient knowledge of English (or even Welsh or Scottish Gaelic) and has stayed out of trouble with the law. The spouse of a British citizen can become naturalized after three years' residency.

Medical requirements   You do not need to show vaccination certificates in order to enter Britain unless you have come from an infected area (some parts of Asia, Africa, and South America, for instance). The only disease you are likely to pick up while in England is a cold. However, immigrants and long-staying visitors and students will be asked to have a tuberculosis vaccination (a shot, not just a test) if they haven't already had one.

Insurance   Most travelers take out general insurance policies that include medical coverage abroad. Something of this sort should be adequate for your medical expenses while in England. The National Health Service (see pp. 194–5) used to be free for everyone, including visitors, but now officially is free only for legal residents and visitors from countries that have reciprocal agreements with Britain (the U.S.A. isn't one of them). However, if you fall ill or have an accident, you *will* receive treatment, and may end up paying only for prescribed medication.

Pets

You *cannot* bring your pet (or a wild animal) with you to Britain unless the animal has first been subjected to a six-month quarantine period. Although this is hard on the beast and expensive for you, the reason is that Britain is one of the few places left that is free from rabies, and it would like to keep things that way. Fines are very heavy for trying to sneak animals into the country, and the poor creature will be sent back immediately or destroyed if discovered.

Duty-free allowance

Many people worry about the amount of goods they are going to take back home with them but don't realize that there are also restrictions on the amount and type of goods they can take *into* another country. Apart from obviously prohibited goods like drugs and weapons, you cannot bring into England certain plants and vegetables, meat, pornography, or articles made from rare animals (such as snow-leopard coats or elephant-foot umbrella stands). However, the restrictions affecting most tourists apply to alcohol, tobacco, and perfume. Duty-free allowances for these substances are complicated and change from time to time, so it is important to find out current restrictions before you leave home. Restrictions are spelled out (in several languages) at ports of entry, but by then it may be too late to hide that extra bottle of booze!

The 1986 allowances for goods are as shown below. Note that you cannot mix allowances from the two columns for the same type of goods. The countries of the EC are Belgium, Denmark, France, West Germany, Greece, the Irish Republic, Italy, Luxembourg, the Netherlands, Portugal, Spain, and the United Kingdom (but not the Channel Islands).

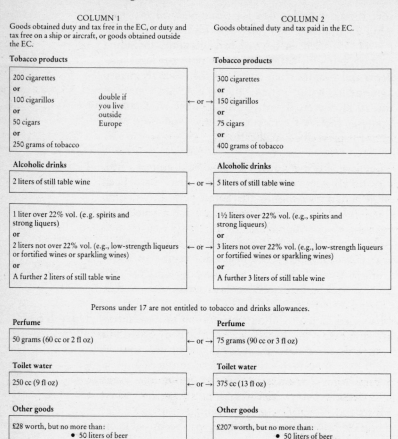

COLUMN 1

Goods obtained duty and tax free in the EC, or duty and tax free on a ship or aircraft, or goods obtained outside the EC.

COLUMN 2

Goods obtained duty and tax paid in the EC.

Tobacco products

200 cigarettes
or
100 cigarillos   double if
or   you live
50 cigars   outside
or   Europe
250 grams of tobacco

← or →

Tobacco products

300 cigarettes
or
150 cigarillos
or
75 cigars
or
400 grams of tobacco

Alcoholic drinks

2 liters of still table wine

← or →

Alcoholic drinks

5 liters of still table wine

1 liter over 22% vol. (e.g. spirits and strong liquers)
or
2 liters not over 22% vol. (e.g., low-strength liqueurs or fortified wines or sparkling wines)
or
A further 2 liters of still table wine

← or →

1½ liters over 22% vol. (e.g., spirits and strong liquers)
or
3 liters not over 22% vol. (e.g., low-strength liqueurs or fortified wines or sparkling wines)
or
A further 3 liters of still table wine

Persons under 17 are not entitled to tobacco and drinks allowances.

Perfume

50 grams (60 cc or 2 fl oz)

← or →

Perfume

75 grams (90 cc or 3 fl oz)

Toilet water

250 cc (9 fl oz)

← or →

Toilet water

375 cc (13 fl oz)

Other goods

£28 worth, but no more than:
• 50 liters of beer
• 25 Mechanical lighters

← or →

Other goods

£207 worth, but no more than:
• 50 liters of beer
• 25 Mechanical lighters

Getting there Since Great Britain is an island, you have to either fly there or float there.

By air Most tourists flying to England land at one of London's two main airports, Heathrow and Gatwick. The London area does have two other airports, Luton and Stansted (mainly used for charter flights), and there are international airports in many other parts of the country that take both scheduled and charter flights from the Americas and the Continent.

The amount of luggage you are allowed to bring with *Luggage*
you on the plane varies according to whether or not
you are on an intercontinental flight and whether it is
a scheduled or charter flight. Transatlantic passengers
are normally allowed two pieces of luggage of a
certain size or weight. However, internal and European flights often limit passengers to one piece of
luggage of a certain weight. It is best to ask your
travel agent or the airline for such information when
planning your trip, especially if you will be traveling
to several countries. Otherwise, you may get stuck
paying for excess baggage.

Many airlines do not let you take garment bags on
board as hand baggage.

Heathrow is one of the busiest airports in the world, **Heathrow**
and you won't need anyone to convince you of this **Airport**
fact if you land there in the middle of the summer. At
various times of the year, especially autumn and late
winter, it is prone to being fogged in in the morning,
so be prepared for delays then, or take a flight that
arrives in the afternoon.

The airport now has four terminals. Terminal 1 is
used by British and Irish airlines for domestic and
European flights; Terminal 2 is for European airlines;
Terminal 3 takes intercontinental flights; and the new
Terminal 4 handles British Airways long-haul flights,
plus BA flights to Paris and KLM to Amsterdam.

If you arrive at Terminal 3 or 4, you may have to walk *Formalities*
for what seems miles before coming to the arrival hall
(there are moving sidewalks part of the way). Once
there, you must join one of the three queues (lines),
depending on what passport you hold: British, EC,
or other. In the summer there is also a line for North
American flights. These queues can take well over 30
minutes to get through if you are unlucky enough to
land at the same time as several jumbo jets. (Get used
to queuing early on, as it is a feature of the English
way of life.) Non-British husbands, wives, or children of British passport holders can usually go
through the British queue with that person if they ask

"Waddya mean, you'll complain
about me to the captain? I am
the captain"

politely at the desk. Terminals 1 and 2 work in the
same manner, but on a smaller scale.

At the passport desk you have to show your
passport and the landing card that you should have
filled out on the plane. You'll be asked why you've
come to the country (business, pleasure, etc.) and
how long you intend to stay. It is sad to have to say
that if you are not white, you may be asked additional
questions or given a warning about overstaying your
visit.

In the baggage area, you can get a free luggage
trolley (baggage cart) if you're quick. These have

brakes that are operated by pressing up on the bar under the handle. After collecting your luggage, you go through one of the two customs channels: *red* if you have something to declare or pay duty on, *green* if you don't. Be warned that the customs officials randomly check the luggage of people going through the green channel.

After passing through customs, you walk through a large doorway to be confronted by the disappointed faces of crowds of people – all hoping that you were the person they were waiting for!

Services

In the main lobby there are various services available, including car hire (rental), accommodation booking, train and bus information, and money-changing facilities. There is also a book and souvenir shop and some food services that are fairly good. Telephones are equipped for international calls, and some even take credit cards (see pp. 37–40).

Terminals 1, 2, and 3 are connected by walkways, and all four by a free yellow shuttle bus. You can get to Gatwick Airport from Heathrow by bus from Terminal 1.

Leaving

When flying abroad from Heathrow, allow plenty of time for checking in during the summer or at Christmastime, as there can be huge queues at the counters. It can also take much longer nowadays to clear the security check, since tighter controls have been brought in. Also leave extra time if you plan to claim tax exemption at the customs desk for goods purchased in Britain (see pp. 119–20).

Getting into London

Heathrow Airport is about 17 miles (27 kilometers) west of London. There are several ways of getting into London from the airport, depending on how much money you want to spend and how much luggage you have. The trip to central London takes 40 to 50 minutes.

Taxis are an expensive choice, but also the most flexible. You can ask the driver to show you some of sights on the way in if you have the time.

Heathrow is also connected to central London by

the Underground (see pp. 60–2) on the Piccadilly line. The trains run every few minutes, from 5 a.m. to 11:45 p.m. on weekdays and 6:45 a.m. to 11 p.m. on Sundays. The trip is relatively inexpensive and is, of course, unaffected by traffic conditions. A disadvantage is that you have to carry your luggage quite a way to reach the Underground (there are some moving sidewalks, and it is all under cover) and then must find space for your bags on the train.

Several buses also serve Heathrow. Red double-decker buses leave for Victoria and Paddington stations from each terminal about every 20 minutes, from 6:30 a.m. to 10:45 p.m. The trip is slower than on the Underground, but there is luggage space provided and you do get to see some of London on the way. Other buses leave from the Central Station at the airport and make several stops along the way. RailAir Link buses leave every 20 minutes from each terminal for the train stations in Reading (for trains going west), Woking (for trains going south), and Watford Junction (for trains going north) Long-distance buses (called coaches; see p. 58) also leave from the terminals and the Central Station, going to most parts of the country.

Most of the services mentioned above are not as frequent on Sundays.

Gatwick Airport Gatwick Airport is about 30 miles (50 kilometers) south of London. The best ways to get into London from there are by one of the frequent trains to Victoria Station, taking about 30 minutes, or by express bus to Victoria, which leaves every half hour until 8 p.m. Trains and buses also leave from Gatwick for a variety of other destinations.

By sea Those who can afford a cruise can arrive in England in style. For non-transatlantic journeys, there are many choices of ferry operator and port of entry. While almost all cross-Channel, North Sea, and Irish Sea ferries take cars, other facilities vary with the operator and length of journey. You can buy food and a limited range of duty-free goods, and use the money-changing facilities on these boats; on longer journeys you can book sleeping accommodation (but do this ahead of time). Ferries that meet up with trains are not as luxurious as others, catering more to economy travelers like students. Note that on most ferries there are seldom lockers for foot passengers to store their luggage in.

The hovercraft, which rides on a cushion of air, cuts the crossing time at least in half, but is not recommended for those prone to sea sickness. It operates only between Calais (in France) and Dover; Boulogne (in France) and Dover; and Boulogne and Ramsgate. The jetfoil, which rises up on what looks like stilts, is also this fast but does not take cars. It runs only between Ostend (in Belgium) and Dover. It is best to book for these in advance.

Most ports are served by trains for further travel in Britain. In the summer, car passengers may have to suffer long, slow queues at the English customs office, where you can be made to feel anything but welcome. The port towns themselves tend to be old and steeped in history, and many are very picturesque.

Remember that while the English Channel is narrow – France is only 20 miles from Dover, and you can see to the other side on a clear day – the sea can get quite rough, especially in the autumn and winter. There are now definite plans for a cross-Channel tunnel, but it is still a very long way off. Besides, many English people are quite happy *not* to be connected to the Continent!

Where to stay

Booking a room

When traveling at the height of the tourist season to popular spots, it is best to book (reserve) your accommodation ahead of time. If you don't, you will probably be able to find a place to stay, but it may not be near where you want to be or the type and price of lodging that you would prefer. Seaside and rural hotels may close for the winter, some as early as October.

The British Tourist Authority (see the Appendix) will send information to you about various kinds of accommodation for a specified area, including inexpensive lodgings if you ask for them. You can, of course, rely on luck, guidebooks, and the hotel accommodation services at airports and large train stations for last-minute arrangements if you can't or don't want to plan ahead of time. Tourist Information Centres (signposted with a white *i* on a blue background), which can be found in most big cities and popular tourist locations, will book accommodation for you for that night or a day ahead for a small fee. However, they may not be open on Saturdays and certainly won't be on Sundays. If at the end of the day you find yourself without a place to lay your head, ask at the nearest pub – the locals are usually friendly and helpful.

It is a good idea to state special preferences or needs concerning your room when making a booking. For example, there is often a quieter side of the building or one aspect with a nicer view. Some hotels have only a few rooms with private baths and toilets, and if you can't get one of those, you may want to be near to or far from the shared facilities. Some places will provide for special dietary needs if told in advance.

Many rooms intended for two people have twin beds, which isn't terribly romantic, so request a double room if you want a double bed. If you ask for an extra *cot* for a child, you will be given a baby's cot; you'd want a *camp bed* or folding bed for an older child or extra adult.

If you have a reservation, you will be expected to arrive by 6 p.m. or to phone to say approximately when you will be arriving. When checking in, you do not need to hand over your passport as you do in many other countries. You should leave your room key at the reception desk whenever you go out.

The standard and quality of accommodation in England vary enormously. It is perfectly all right, and can be a good idea, to ask to see a room before you take it.

What to expect
Facilities

The AA (Automobile Association) and RAC (Royal Automobile Club) rate places of accommodation according to a system of stars that relates to the number of amenities (and not necessarily to the level of comfort and pleasantness of surroundings). One-star premises are very basic but clean, and five-star locations are extremely nice and expensive. Don't expect to find a swimming pool unless you go to a top-notch establishment. Any place receiving an AA or RAC rating will display the stars on its sign; there are also books available that list rated premises (see Appendix for AA and RAC addresses).

One- and two-star establishments usually don't have private bathrooms or toilets. Even in rooms that don't have these, you will almost always find a handbasin (sink) with hot and cold water. Shared facilities are generally clean, but you are expected to rinse out the bathtub after using it. Showers are not all that common in hotels, so you may have to ask for a hand hose for washing your hair.

Always remember to bring a face flannel (wash cloth) with you when traveling in England, because you won't be provided with one in your room (except in American-style hotels). Using a washcloth that someone else has used before is seen as being just about as unthinkable as using another person's toothbrush! Fortunately, there is no such taboo about towels.

Most hotels and motels have dining facilities and are licensed (to serve alcohol). You will, of course, find excellent facilities and well-appointed surroundings in the expensive luxury and first-class hotels, most of which are found in London and in the major tourist centers. Other classes of accommodation, however, may not have central heating, private bathrooms, or televisions in every room (if they do, they will advertise these facts on their signs). Older buildings might lack elevators and well-maintained decor and furnishings.

Being looked after
Hotels

It is hard to generalize about hotels, since they range from huge resort establishments to small converted houses, from centuries-old buildings with open fireplaces to modern chains with discos. Those hotels that hold the most attraction for visitors are usually old properties that have been modernized but still retain their charm and atmosphere. Staying in a real Tudor building, hunting lodge, or manor house adds something special to a holiday.

The larger, more expensive hotels usually have a formal, sophisticated air. Smaller hotels are often run by families on a more informal basis; in fact, in some you may actually feel obligated to chat with the proprietors.

Guest houses

Guest houses are roughly the English equivalent of the European *pensions*. They tend to be relatively inexpensive, family-run, small hotels in converted houses. They may or may not provide meals other than breakfast and will probably not have a bar. Bathroom facilities more often than not are shared, although there may be a sink in the room. Beware in London and large cities, for some guest houses are in poor condition and are located in seedy areas, or may be used to house large numbers of homeless people.

B&Bs

Bed-and-breakfast (B&B) establishments are just that: inexpensive places to sleep, with breakfast included. But you are expected *not* to hang around during the day. B&Bs are usually just ordinary families' houses with a few spare rooms, located in normal residential areas. While this gives you an excellent opportunity to meet local people, you can also feel like you are intruding into their private lives. You may have a wonderful – or an uncomfortable stay – do ask to see the room before you commit yourself. In the country, farmhouses often advertise B&B.

There are relatively few motels yet, but they tend to be bright and clean, even if they do lack character.   *Motels*

In the olden days, travelers relied on inns along the main stagecoach routes for food, drink, and lodging. Today, many of these inns still serve the same purpose. It is hard to pass up the combination of a pub, restaurant, and hotel located in a characterful building several centuries old. Inns have many charms, but they also have their drawbacks: floors may creak, bathrooms will often be shared, and there can be a lot of noise until the restaurant and pub close.   *Inns and pubs*

   Country pubs usually have several rooms above the main bar, which provides a chance for inexpensive accommodation as well as a watering hole near at hand. Rooms tend to be clean but small and basic, and bathroom and toilet facilities are almost always shared. Some pubs offer meals, but many serve only snacks.

Room prices should be displayed in the lobby. Rates vary according to the number of facilities *en suite* and the number of people using the room. You may get a reduced rate for a child sharing the room, although this practice is not standard everywhere.   *Price*

   The better hotels in London are some of the most expensive in Europe. There are nice London hotels that don't cost an arm and a leg, but those on the cheaper end of the scale can be somewhat shabby. It isn't a bad idea to leave your luggage somewhere safe (e.g., in a locker in one of the large train stations), go to the area of London you want to stay in, and walk around until you find a place that suits your needs and pocketbook. You may actually find it cheaper to stay just outside of London and take a train in each day.

VAT (value added tax), which is currently 15 percent, is added on to the bill for the room. If you've had good service (and a service charge hasn't been put on the bill), a 10 percent tip paid with the bill would be welcome. Larger hotels accept major credit cards, and many now take British traveler's cheques (checks). Foreign currency and foreign traveler's checks are usually taken only by large hotels in popular tourist spots.

Porters expect a tip of 50 pence to £1, depending on how much luggage you've made them carry.

Meals   Breakfast is included in the price of most rooms, although in London this doesn't always hold true. The more traditional establishments will also either provide tea-making facilities in each room or bring morning tea and a newspaper to your door before breakfast. The English breakfast is an awesome affair, consisting of juice, fruit, cold cereal or hot porridge, then either smoked fish or grilled bacon, sausage, eggs, mushrooms and tomatoes, all followed by toast and marmalade, with tea or coffee. Many places also offer a Continental breakfast (juice, a roll, and coffee or tea), sometimes with a boiled egg. (Some will bring Continental breakfast to your room if you prefer.)

Meals are generally served between set (and somewhat restricted) times, so you can't expect to get up at 10:00 and have breakfast or to have your dinner at 5:30. Room service is usually available only at plush hotels. If you want to spend the day in the countryside, many places will make you a 'packed lunch' if you ask the night before. Smaller and more rural hotels often expect you to eat dinner there, and you should tell the proprietor early in the day if you won't be dining in. Some of the best English cooking can be found at country hotels.

Looking after yourself
Youth hostels

Despite the name, youth hostels are not just for the young. To use them, you need a current Youth Hostel membership card (you can get one in England; see the Appendix). The price per night is very low, partly because everyone has to help with domestic chores. Some hostels are self-catering (you cook your own food); others provide cheap meals; most offer the choice. Accommodation is dormitory-style, with between four and twenty beds per room – and *no* mixing of sexes allowed. Blankets are provided, but not bed linen. You must bring either a sheet sleeping sack or an ordinary sleeping bag; some hostels rent sheet sacks. The longest you can stay at any particular hostel is three days; and you have to go out during the day between 10:00 and 5:00. There is usually a curfew at night (quite early) for the benefit of early-rising hikers.

Universities

Some universities rent out rooms during vacation periods. Meals may be provided, but often there are shared kitchen facilities for guests. Rooms are single-occupancy only and tend to be adequate but very small. Bathroom facilities are shared, although there may be a handbasin in the room. University grounds are usually very pleasant.

Boats

Canal and river boats provide a more unusual type of self-catering accommodation. England has several thousand miles of inland waterways to explore, giving you a chance to enjoy scenery and wildlife that you just can't see from the roads. You can rent boats of various sizes with all facilities aboard, but it is wise to book a boat in advance (get a brochure from a travel agent). You don't have to be experienced to pilot a canal boat – it doesn't go very fast, and you will be given instructions on how to run the boat and negotiate any locks. You are allowed to moor only at designated spots. Mooring is at a premium near built-up areas and waterside pubs in the summer and spring holiday periods.

Camping and caravanning

Camping out in a tent is probably less popular in England than in many other countries, largely because of the unpredictable weather. However, England does have many designated campsites, some of which are in the national parks. There are guidebooks listing these sites and their amenities, and

Tourist Information Centres can also guide you to good camping areas. Tenting is mainly restricted to these campsites, but in the open countryside you may camp freely on uncultivated land, unless told otherwise. If you ask nicely, farmers may allow you to camp in their meadows.

Caravan (trailer) holidays are also available, for which you rent a fully equipped caravan on a particular site, often near the seaside. However, these sites can be crowded and many destroy the beauty of their locations. Some sites are quite luxurious, while others have few facilities. If you bring your own caravan at the height of the season, you should reserve a spot at a site well ahead of time. Again, there are several guidebooks that list locations. You are not allowed to park caravans overnight in lay-bys (parking turnouts) next to the road. If you do see a group of caravans at the side of the road and don't see a camping sign, then the site is most likely inhabited by a group of Gypsies or similar itinerant people.

Staying in a house

You can hire (rent out) fully furnished holiday properties, and several books, magazines, and newspapers carry advertisements for such self-catering accommodations (check in newsagents, see p. 123). These run the gamut from modern luxury London flats to seaside bungalows, isolated cottages, farmhouses, Georgian mansions, and most everything in between, including converted railway stations, schoolhouses, and even windmills. Most have to be rented for at least a week. If there is a phone in the house, you probably won't have the use of it; you'll have to go out to find a public telephone (see p. 37).

If you are staying in an English house as a guest, a small gift of candy, liquor, or flowers for your hosts would be appropriate, although not necessarily expected. Don't use the phone without asking, as there is a charge even for local calls.

The English house

English houses encompass an enormous and interesting range of styles and ages. (The word *home* is not used for the physical building but is reserved for the abstract concept; also, a *home* is where you keep the decrepit, the delirious, and the delinquent.) In general, English houses have a cozy rather than a spacious feel to them. Most housing is terraced (row house) or semi-detached (duplex), even, surprisingly, in country areas. Terraces range from luxurious and grand rows in wealthy parts of big cities to depressingly cramped workers' housing. Semi-detached houses are usually a good size, although they are sometimes bungalows (single-story dwellings). Detached houses (those standing on their own) are not as common, probably because of the lack of living space relative to the size of the population.

In cities and towns of any size, you can find flats (self-contained apartments), maisonettes (flats extending over more than one floor), and bed-sits (one-room units with shared facilities). These may be in converted large houses or in newer blocks of flats (apartment complexes). Cities have experimented with tower blocks (high-rise apartment buildings), but the people forced to live in them found them fairly undesirable, and they aren't being built anymore.

The term *cottage* may conjure up the image of a small, white, thatched country dwelling, but in fact it refers to many different kinds of house, both small and large, old and new, rural and urban, detached and attached. Old cottages are lovely and quaint, but unless they've been modernized, they can also be damp, dark, and drafty. And if you're large or tall, beware: low ceilings, tiny rooms, and narrow hallways may reduce your comfort considerably.

Most houses, no matter what size, will have a 'garden,' so called even if it has room for only one plant or is just grass. Gardens are one of the delights of England. Even the tiniest of front gardens is usually colorful and surrounded by a fence, low wall, or hedge (to stake out one's territory), while back gardens may include a lawn, flower beds, shrubs and often vegetables, and typically have higher barricades around them (for privacy). Never make fun of English people's gardens – they are their pride and joy, often deservedly so.

Many houses, especially the older terraced ones, do

"Beautiful! Such understatement!"

Drawing by Saxon; © 1966 The New Yorker Magazine, Inc.,
is reproduced by kind permission

not have garages. The garages there are tend to be just
large enough to squeeze in a small car. They are often
detached from the house and may not have electricity.

Heating   Whatever time of year you go to England, take along
a sweater. Even if you don't need it outdoors, you
may need it indoors.

Many English houses were built before insulation
was thought of, and many built afterward simply
don't have it. A good number of house owners have
now insulated their lofts (attics) and walls and have
installed double glazing (double-paned windows;
screens aren't necessary in most areas). Damp in
houses is sometimes a problem, however.

A typical older house has small rooms that are
locally heated, although central heating is also common. Doors are an integral part of the heating system;
only the room being used is heated and all doors
leading from it are kept tightly shut. It is unforgivable
to leave a door ajar or to go in and out of a heated
room several times unnecessarily. Long, thin 'sausage' pillows are sometimes put in front of doors to

keep drafts from whistling through, and long, heavy curtains (drapes) are used to try to trap cold air coming from drafty windows. Of course, newer and modernized houses do not suffer from these problems. Some houses, both old and new, have no heating in the kitchen or the room with the toilet.

Fireplaces are widely found in the main living room, although gas fires have replaced real ones in many houses. Electric 'fires,' which are space heaters with two or three heating bars, are common but not very efficient, as they heat only a very small space and are expensive to run. Those found in bathrooms are placed high up on the wall so that the ceiling is nicely warmed while you freeze in the tub! Oil-filled electric radiators are also expensive to run. A cheaper system is the electric storage heater, which stores heat during cheap electricity rate periods and releases it later. You must predict how much heat to store for any given day, however, and if you need more heat you must have a different type of heater on hand for backup. Central heating is the norm in new houses and many older ones – an oil, gas or solid fuel boiler is operated by a central thermostat (often in the hall) and time clock.

Some heaters (and the entire electrical system in some houses) are operated by coin-fed meters, most of which use either 10 pence or 50 pence coins.

Electricity

The electric current in English houses is 220 or 240 volts. This is incompatible with North American and Japanese appliances, so don't bring any unless you also bring a voltage adaptor. The higher voltage makes it much easier to electrocute yourself, and to remedy this state of affairs, the power points (electric outlets) have on-off switches. For many tourists from North America, this causes two main problems: first, the switches work in reverse order (down for 'on', up for 'off'); and second, it is hard to remember to turn on nonlight switches. You can spend ages wondering why the heater isn't heating up, or, even worse, why the roast isn't roasting, before realizing that you haven't turned on the relevant switch.

If you are used to having an electric outlet on most

walls, you will find English rooms very frustrating. Unless the house is new or has been rewired, there is often only one double socket per room (and none in the bathroom because of the danger of electrocution). This leads to the overloading of outlets, with multiple sockets plugged into other multiple sockets and yards of extension cord strung around the room. (See pp. 124–5 for how to put on plugs.)

Electric meters are often located inside houses in fairly inaccessible places (like under the stairs in a cupboard), although newer electric and gas meters are located outside. If the meter-reader can't get in when he calls, your bill may be estimated – you can get this corrected if you like. There are no water meters, as charges consist of a flat rate.

Kitchens   Most English kitchens are not as elaborately equipped as, say, American or Scandinavian ones. Microwave ovens, dishwashers, trash compactors, heavy-duty garbage disposals, and small extravagances such as electric can openers are not found in the average English kitchen. If there is a garbage disposal, it may handle only soft items such as tea leaves and vegetable peelings.

One standard – and wonderful – appliance is the electric kettle, which heats water up very quickly. Newer ones have a button on the handle that must be pressed in to activate them (after you remember to switch on the socket). The kettles with buttons turn themselves off when the water boils; the older ones just continue to boil until you unplug them or turn off the socket. Electric kettles do not whistle when they boil.

Cookers (stoves) usually have a separate grill (broiler) above the oven, sometimes at eye level on gas cookers. Older gas cookers do not have a pilot light, making it necessary to use matches or a special sparking lighter to get them started; newer ones may have an ignitor button. Aga cookers (which are fairly rare) burn coke or solid fuel.

Newer electric cookers have temperatures marked in centigrade, so a conversion chart may be necessary for those who have failed to learn the metric system (see p. 205). Many English recipes give amounts of dry ingredients by weight rather than by volume, so a set of kitchen scales is a standard item (usually marked off in both Imperial and metric amounts).

Refrigerators are often small, some fitting under a counter, with very little freezer space, although larger ones are becoming more common. Kitchen sinks are often single-basin ones, so plastic basins are put in for washing up dishes. The English tend not to rinse their dishes. Sinks usually do not have mixer taps.

Other items you might find in an English kitchen include a tea trolley, which is a double-decker tray on wheels, used for carting around all the tea goodies; tea cozies and egg cozies, which are like little quilted or knitted hats that fit over teapots and boiled eggs to keep them warm; and toast racks.

Laundry

Since English houses usually don't have a basement or utility room, clothes washers and dryers are often located in the kitchen under a counter. Many people still have semi-automatic washers, which have to be filled through a hose attached to the kitchen taps (faucets) and drained into the sink. Tumble dryers are not as common as spin dryers. Most people seem content with hanging clothes outside to dry or draping them all over the house. Hanging them outside can be a very optimistic gesture, as you can't depend on the weather staying the same. However, the sunshine is free, while large appliances can be expensive.

Bathrooms

If you ask for the bathroom in England (or in any European country), you will probably be shown the room with the bath tub in it; there will not necessarily be a toilet in the same room. Americans find it difficult to bring themselves to ask for the 'toilet,' but that is what it is called. (Other polite terms include 'lavatory' and 'loo'.) There will be a washbasin or handbasin in the bathroom, but not always in the room with the toilet.

If you enjoy taking showers, you may be disappointed in an English house. Plumbing was put into the older houses before showers became fashionable. Even in newer houses, hot water pressure may be too low to allow you to rig up a shower hose from the taps (faucets). Cups or short spray attachments have to be used instead for washing your hair, which can result in your getting a sore back from bending over the sink or tub. Beware of letting the spray head fall into a full tub or sink, for this can cause back-siphoning, which can pollute the water supply. Newer shower systems that run off the cold water supply and instantly heat the water are very much on the increase. The English are very clever at finding places to squeeze in new shower cubicles – bedroom corners and even stairway landings get used.

On the other hand, if you enjoy taking baths, you have come to the right place. Bathtubs are luxuriously deep and long, allowing you to spoil yourself with a leisurely soak. Beware that hot water supplies can be quickly used up.

Bathroom scales are marked off in, believe it or not, *stones*. There are 14 pounds (6.35 kilograms) to one stone, with each pound marked on the scale. So if you weigh 8 1/2 stone, the equivalent is 119 pounds (54 kilograms); 14 stone translates into 196 pounds (89 kilograms).

Don't look for a box of tissues in any room other than the bathroom: handkerchiefs are still the norm.

Bedding   Bedding often consists of a *duvet* (pronounced 'doovay'), a thick eiderdown or fiber quilt encased in a sheeting cover that can be removed for laundering. In warm weather these get rather hot, but you can shake the filling down to the bottom of a feather duvet to make a lighter cover. Sheets and blankets and thin quilts (called eiderdowns) are still usual, particularly among older people. Electric blankets are fairly common. Most are under blankets that are used to warm up the bed and must be turned off before you get in. Where no such luxury exists, the faithful hot water bottle is still used for warming a small part of the bed. Bed socks also sell well.

Storage   Storage space is a real problem in the traditional English house. There is usually no basement. Built-in closets are rare. And the loft (attic) may be difficult to get at. The alternative to having expensive fitted bedroom closets installed is to buy a large, free-standing wardrobe, which leaves little room to move around in a small bedroom. Instead of coat closets in the hallway, many people use a coat stand or a row of hooks on the wall. Many houses have a closet under the stairs, where brooms, ironing-boards and *hoovers* (vacuum cleaners) are stored.

Another type of closet that you will probably find is an *airing cupboard*. This is a sort of linen closet that also contains the hot water heater. Warm air from the heater circulates through the slatted shelves to keep towels and sheets dry and fresh. Some airing cupboards are fitted with rails so that they can be used to dry clothes too.

Curtains often do not have a pull-cord for opening and shutting them; instead, you just grasp the material and pull it along. One advantage of this system is that you can have just one curtain drawn, which isn't possible with a pulley system.

Drapes

Changing light bulbs can be a confusing business. Most English light bulbs do not unscrew – be sure to remember this, or you may end up with a handful of broken glass. They have what is called a *bayonet fitting*. Two metal pins stick out on opposite sides of the bulb where the screw threads on American light bulbs would be. These fit into slots in the lamp base or overhead fixture. To remove a bulb, press the bulb itself in and turn it slightly to the left. To insert a bulb, press the pins into the slots and turn the bulb slightly to the right. The bulb should lock into place. This will all become clear when you see a bayonet fitting face to face.

Lights

Overhead lights are often suspended from the ceiling rather than attached to it. It is not uncommon to see a lampshade or paper lantern, rather than a fancy light fixture, dangling from the cord.

The English do not have garbage cans – they have *dustbins*, which are emptied, of course, by the

Garbage pickup

© Gray Jolliffe 1986. Reproduced from 'Brit-think Ameri-think' by
Jane Walmsley by permission of Harrap Ltd.

dustmen, who come once a week. In many areas the
dustmen leave a large *bin-liner* for each house when
they collect the rubbish. Plastic bags for small indoor
waste containers are also called bin-liners.

Repairs and   If anything goes wrong in a house you're responsible
emergencies   for, e.g. with the plumbing, the central heating, the
gas or the electricity, consult the *Yellow Pages* (see p.
39) for the names and telephone numbers of local
plumbers, builders or the gas or electricity boards.
You will also find painters, decorators, double-
glazers etc., in this directory.

Money and banking

The amount of money you bring with you will depend, of course, on your length of stay and style of living. Visitors from many countries, however, may find everyday items in London to be more expensive than they are at home.

It is a good idea wherever you travel to have at least a small amount of the local currency with you when you arrive in case you immediately need to use a telephone, take a taxi, etc. You can probably get British currency from your bank at home if you ask at least a week in advance of your trip. If not, international airports and ferry ports have foreign exchange facilities but may have a less favorable exchange rate than a bank.

Changing money

Once in England, you will get the best rate of exchange at a bank. It is best to go to larger bank branches when changing foreign currency, as some of the smaller branches do not offer this service. (Do not go to a building society, which is for savings and loans only.) Banking hours are 9:30 a.m. to 3:30 p.m. Monday through Friday (excluding holidays). Some large branches of banks are open on Saturday mornings, but in general, banks are not open on the weekends.

You can buy and sell foreign currency at most Thomas Cook travel agencies and at the many *bureaux de change* in London and other major tourist areas. Many bureaux de change are open late in the evenings and on weekends, but they don't tend to give such good rates as banks do. Some main post offices in tourist areas also function as bureaux de change (look for a sign saying so). Some larger hotels and restaurants in tourist areas will accept major foreign currencies, but do not assume this will be so.

Traveler's cheques (checks)

These are by far the safest way to carry money, for they can be replaced if lost or stolen. However, they are not as convenient to use in England as they are in North America, for they cannot be used to buy things directly but must first be exchanged at a bank for cash. Traveler's checks in pounds sterling are more readily accepted by hotels and shops. Another advantage of pound sterling checks is that they can be exchanged for cash at any bank window, while those in foreign currency have to be handled at the foreign exchange window, which inevitably has a longer line at peak holiday times. When cashing traveler's checks, you will be asked to show some form of identification – your passport will do nicely.

Foreign bank checks

Probably no one in England, except your friends, will accept a check drawn on a foreign bank account.

Visitors from many European countries can use Eurocheques in England much as they would use normal bank checks. However, you must already have the special Eurocheques and Eurocheque card (obtained via your own bank before you leave). You make the check out in pounds sterling, and that amount is deducted from your bank account at home at the current exchange rate.

Visitors with post office Giro accounts from Denmark, France, Luxembourg, the Netherlands, and Norway can cash Postcheques at main post offices and branches displaying the Postcheque sign.

Credit cards

Most major credit cards are honored in restaurants and stores in England; look for signs in the window. Many petrol (gas) stations also accept credit cards, but note that petrol companies do *not* issue or accept special oil company credit cards as they do in the U.S. and Canada.

Access (MasterCard) and Visa credit cards can be used to obtain money from British banks, up to a daily limit of £50. If you have an American Express card, you will be able to write a check in dollars or change a traveler's check for up to £50 at any American Express office.

Your signature on a credit card slip will be checked

Reproduced by permission of *Private Eye*

against that on the back of the card, so don't lend your card to another family member – it won't work. Credit card transactions will be billed to you at home at the current rate of exchange.

British currency

Britain has had a decimal currency system since 1971, when it abandoned (somewhat reluctantly) the puzzling old system of shillings, florins, half crowns, and guineas (there were 20 shillings or 240 old pence to the pound). Now the pound sterling (written £) consists of 100 new pence (written *p*).

British coins tend to be quite heavy (or substantial, as the British prefer to think of them). Most foreigners end up with a lot of loose change and thus have heavy handbags or drooping trousers, so try your best to spend the coins.

All coins have a picture of the sovereign on the front (the Queen nowadays). The current coins are:

1p   copper, small
2p   copper, larger for its value
5p   silver, smaller than the 2p (older coins say *one shilling*)
10p silver, larger, very heavy (older coins say *two shillings*)

20p silver, small, light, 7-sided (easily confused
     with a 5p)
50p silver, large, very heavy, 7-sided
£1   gold, just smaller than the 5p, very thick

(The ½p coin, copper and very small, is no longer
legal tender, so don't bother bringing any with
you.)

The notes vary in size and color, which makes it
very easy to identify the denominations quickly.
However, the larger ones don't fit very well into slim
wallets. The notes that you are most likely to see are:

£5   blue
£10 brown
£20 purple
£50 yellowish-brown

(The green £ note is no longer being printed and is not
legal tender anymore.)

Scottish and Northern Ireland banks, and the
Channel Islands, are allowed to issue their own coins
and notes, which differ in design from bank to bank.
Some English people may refuse to accept them;
however, a bank is obliged to change them.

The term *quid* is slang for a pound. *Pence* is often
abbreviated to *p* in speech as well as writing. An
amount such as £5.50 is spoken as 'five pounds fifty
(pence),' not 'five and a half pounds.' Sometimes shop
assistants (clerks) say amounts just over £1 in pence –
e.g., £1.08 as 'a hundred and eight pence'. *Bob* refers
to the old shilling (10 bob equals 50 new pence). If
you hear someone refer to an amount like 'four and
six,' they are reverting to the old nondecimal system
(that is, four shillings and sixpence, or 22½ new
pence).

**Bank
accounts**

The following information is for those who are
staying in England long enough to make it worth-
while getting a bank account.

There are only about half a dozen major banking
companies in England. The Post Office also has a
regular banking service, called Girobank (see p. 36).
Some banks will ask you for the names of two people

in England as references in order for you to open an account.

There are two types of bank account: current (checking) and deposit (savings).

Current accounts

A current account is usually a noninterest account. It is most useful after you have been given a bank-guaranteed check card, which can take as long as three to six months after opening your account. (It takes that long for some people to prove they are reliable.) Armed with this card and your check book, you can write checks anywhere a personal check is accepted (which is most places: restaurants, shops, petrol (gas) stations, post offices, etc.) and can withdraw up to £50 a day from *any* bank in the country. There may be a charge for cashing a check at a bank other than your own; also, you have to present your check book so that the bank clerk (teller) can mark off the date in the back to prevent you from cheating on the daily limit.

Without a check card, your checks will probably not be accepted for goods or services. You can, of course, cash checks at your own bank branch without the card, but other banks may telephone your bank first and charge you for the call. You can deposit money into your account from any bank in the country at no charge (even without a bank card) by filling out a bank Giro slip.

Checks are either open or crossed (with two vertical lines running through the blank horizontal ones). Crossed checks are safer as they must be deposited into the payee's account and thus can't be cashed if lost or stolen. You can endorse a check anywhere you like on the back. Remember that when writing the date in numerals, you put the day before the month; thus June 10, 1986, would be 10/6/86.

Your current account balance statement will come once every three months, or more often if you ask, but canceled checks will not be returned to you. You can ask at the bank for your balance at any time.

If you overdraw your account, you will eventually receive a polite letter from the bank calling this fact to your attention and suggesting that you might wish to do something about it. The bank will pay on overdrawn checks (unless they are for unreasonable amounts) and will deduct the interest on this instant loan from your account. It's very civilized.

Giro accounts

Post Office Giro accounts work like regular bank accounts, with a few different restrictions on check cashing. Having your account with the Post Office has certain advantages: post offices are open longer than banks, including Saturday mornings, and they are located even in small, remote villages.

Money machines

Many banks now have automatic money-dispensing machines at their main branches, which work via a special bank card and a secret number (you can easily apply for a card if you have an account). Most cardholders find these machines very handy, although queues are quite long on evenings and weekends, and the machines often seem to break down or run out of money just when you need to use one! Many such machines also give balance statements, transfer money from one account to another, and provide other services.

Keeping in touch

Telephones

The Post Office used to be in charge of both the postal service and the telephone service, which is why post boxes and call boxes (telephone booths) were both painted the same deep red color. However, this marriage of the communication services was broken up in 1981 and the private British Telecom (BT) company now runs the phone service. In trying to gradually upgrade equipment, BT is replacing those much-loved and traditional sturdy call boxes with what it hopes will be vandal-proof ones. These new metal contraptions have no doors, which makes it no great pleasure to phone someone on a cold, windy day from a noisy street. Many people would prefer BT to turn their attention more quickly to improving the quality of the telephone connections. Often lines seem to be plagued by crackling noises, fading signals, or voices in the background; the connection may improve if you dial the number again. International calls can deteriorate to the point where you can barely hear the other person, although sometimes they are much clearer than local calls.

Tones

The various official telephone sounds are:

dial tone: a continuous hum
number ringing: a repeated double burr
number engaged (busy): a repeated single tone
number unobtainable (out of order; nonexistent):
    a continuous note

An 'engaged' tone can sometimes mean that the exchange you are contacting, rather than the number, is engaged – so try again.

Public phones

About 20 percent of British households are still not 'on the phone.' Because of this, call boxes are scattered throughout residential, shopping, and country areas. They can also be found outside most post offices and in pubs. They tend to be in working order, but those that do break down or get vandalized are not repaired very quickly. If a call box has a '999 calls only' sign on it, that means you can call only the emergency services (free of charge) from that telephone. The minimum charge for other calls is 10p at present.

Coin-operated

The older-style dial pay phones (in red call-boxes) are steadily being replaced by new push-button versions. The older ones only take 10p coins. To use one, lift the receiver and dial the number you want (but don't dial too quickly). If someone answers, you will hear a series of rapid *pips*. Push your coin into the slot, and the pips will stop. When your time is up, the pips will start again; just feed in more coins to continue the call.

The new pay phones allow you to use a wider range of coins, which means you don't have to carry around a sack of 10p pieces to make a long-distance or international call. Some of these take 2p, 10p, and 50p coins only, while others take any British coin except the 1p. To use one, put your money in before dialing. While you talk, a digital display tells you how much money you have left so that you can insert more before your time runs out. Any coin that hasn't been used at the end of your call will be returned (but not change from a partially used coin).

Not all pay phones will accept incoming calls, so check to see if there is a sign to that effect before asking someone to ring you back.

Credit cards

Pay phones that don't require any coins at all are also being phased in. At airports and large train stations you can find some that take major credit cards; these tend to be more expensive per minute than normal pay phones.

Phonecard

A new invention of British Telecom is the Phonecard. These come in a specified number of 10p units (20, 40, 100, or 200) and can be bought at post offices and from many newsagents (see p. 123). As you talk, the digital display on the phone tells you how many units you have left on the card. Phonecards can be used only in call boxes that carry a green Phonecard sign. These are on the increase, and usually are found where there are several pay phones together (e.g., at airports, train stations, and major shopping areas).

One problem with all pay phones is that you have to estimate how much money to insert. There is no indication of what the rate per minute is, and rates vary with the time of day and distance of the call in any case. At present, 10p buys about 5 minutes of a local call. The cheapest rates for domestic calls are between 6 p.m. and 8 a.m. on weekdays, and all weekend long. The most expensive time to make a call is between 9 a.m. and 1 p.m. The cheapest international rate is between 8 p.m. and 8 a.m., and all weekend. *Rates*

There are two main telephone directories – one listing private numbers (and also British Rail, schools, some shops, banks, doctors' surgeries etc.,) in alphabetical order; and the *Yellow Pages* containing a list of local businesses in alphabetical order of type of business. British telephone numbers consist of a town exchange name and/or area code in parentheses, followed by the local number, e.g., Norwich (0603) 12334. The number of digits included in the codes and numbers varies, usually from three to six numerals each. When dialing a number with the same exchange as the phone you are using (that is, in the same town or immediate area), simply dial the local number. To make a long-distance call, first dial the area code, which always begins with 0. However, if the number you want to ring is neither within the same exchange nor long distance but falls within the 'local dialing area,' then you should use the local dialing code. This consists of one to six numerals and gets you onto a cheaper network than the long-distance one. A dialing code book is issued for each locality (and is included in the front of newer phone books), giving both local and long-distance codes. Call boxes should display local and major national codes, but these are **Phone numbers** sometimes missing or defaced (if so, call directory enquiries for help – see 'operator services' below).

To illustrate the system, let's say you want to ring the following number: Goring-on-Thames 1234. If phoning from Goring, you dial only 1234. If phoning from within the local dialing area, you dial 92–1234. If phoning long distance, you dial 0491–1234.

International calls
Most international calls can be dialed direct, including from pay phones. To dial a foreign number, first dial the international code 010, then the country code (found in the dialing code book), then the number. To dial England from another country, dial that country's international code, then 44 (Britain's code), then the area code minus the initial 0, then the local number.

Operator services
To find out a particular phone number from the operator (telephone books are sometimes missing from call boxes), dial 192 for directory enquiries, free of charge. You can make transferred-charge (collect), person-to-person, or credit-card calls by dialing 100 for the operator. A handy service if you are using someone else's phone is ADC – advice of duration and charge: ask for this before you make your call and the operator will come on the line at the end of the call and tell you how much the call cost. You can also ask the operator for an alarm (wake-up) call.

Emergencies
For emergencies, dial 999 and state which emergency service you need – police, fire department, or ambulance.

Telegrams
International telegrams can be sent by dialing 100 and asking for that service. The Telemessage service, for domestic telegrams, is also reached by dialing 100. You can no longer send a telegram within the U.K. and have it delivered the same day; it will be delivered the next working day, including Saturday, by normal post. For special occasions such as weddings, births, birthdays, etc., the telemessage can be put into a special greeting card.

There are a variety of recorded information services that can be useful or fun to listen to (but they are not free). These include the Speaking Clock (time), weather reports for specific areas, road and rail travel information, sports results, gardening information, recipes, and others, all of which are listed in the phone book. You can even have a bedtime story read over the phone! One very useful service is What's on in London (and What's on in Edinburgh, in the summer only), given in English, French, and German.

Information services

Since the English are often thought of as polite and quaint, you might expect them to use an interesting greeting when answering the phone. Instead, they simply recite their telephone number, without even saying 'Hello.' If you do answer the phone with a greeting, the caller will often ask 'is that . . . ' and recite the number. This strange habit seems to indicate a mistrust (not altogether misplaced perhaps) of the reliability of the telephone service.

Answering the phone

Telephone numbers are read out one digit at a time, except for repeated numerals: 22333 would be 'double two, treble three'; 45555 would be 'four, double five, double five.' And 0 is 'oh,' not 'zero.'

Remember that if you answer the phone and hear rapid pips, it doesn't mean that the phone is broken but that someone is trying to phone from a call box. Be patient and wait for the person to put the money in.

Home phone installation charges are very high, and it can take a long time for the phone company to get around to putting the phone in. You are charged a monthly phone rental cost unless you buy your own phone.

Bills

You are charged for every call made – there is no flat monthly rate for local calls. Phone bills, like other utility bills, come once every three months. Long-distance calls are not itemized on the bill. If you share a phone, you all need to record your calls in order to allocate the bill between you.

Mail   The British postal service delivers mail twice a day Monday through Friday in urban areas, at least once per weekday everywhere else, and once on Saturdays. A first-class letter should reach its destination in England the next day if posted early; second-class mail takes two or three days to get to most areas of the country. For urgent deliveries, services such as Red Star and Datapost are available – you can get information on these at a post office.

Post offices   Post offices are open from 9 a.m. to 5:30 p.m. Monday through Friday and 9 a.m. to 12:30 p.m. on Saturday. The post office at Trafalgar Square in London operates from 8 a.m. to 10 p.m. Monday through Saturday and 10 a.m. to 5 p.m. on Sundays and holidays (except Christmas). Small sub-post offices may close early one day a week (see Shopping, p. 118). Stamp machines are located outside many post offices and sell stamps at the cover price. (Note that no other shops sell stamps, though sometimes card shops will sell you one to go with a card – they can't make a profit on them.)

A large town or city will have a main post office that offers a full range of services. Besides selling stamps and sending parcels, these handle such things as passport and car tax applications, television license payments, pension and child-support payments, and Girobank services. Post offices don't usually sell such items as padded envelopes, tape, or string, nor do they provide wet sponges for moistening stamps and envelope flaps. Small sub-post offices are far more common and offer a restricted range of services. They are usually located in shops such as newsagents, stationers, confectioners, grocers, and tobacconists.

While you are in England, you may want to make use of the free *post restante* service and have letters sent to you at the Head Post Office of whatever town you are in. In larger cities you must find out what the office's postal district is. To collect your mail, just ask at the desk.

Post boxes   The English post their letters in post boxes (also called letter boxes); mail is not left for the postman at houses. The most common sorts of post box are pillar boxes, which are easy to recognize – they are large red cylindrical containers that look like overgrown fire hydrants. Other post boxes are built flush into walls to camouflage them from the public – though they are always red.

Collection times are listed on each box and numbered. When the postmen collect the post, they put up the number for the next collection time – a useful system if you arrive at the box just at a collection time and don't know whether you're in time to catch that post.

When addressing a letter to someone in England, it is very important to include the terms *Street*, *Avenue*, *Road*, etc., since there are often several places with similar names in a town. For example, in London there are Cannon Close, Cannon Hill, Cannon Lane, Cannon Place, Cannon Road, Cannon Row, Cannon Street, and, believe it or not, Cannon Street Road. A house may go by a name (like The Rectory or Rose Cottage) and not have a street number.

Addressing a letter

Small towns and villages may also have a post town in the address, which comes under the town name and should be put in capital letters. (Post towns are given in local telephone directories.)

You should include the county name in the address, although large cities and towns do not need one, and you should *always* include the postcode. Postcodes consist of a combination of five to seven letters and digits divided into two groups; the second group always has one digit followed by two letters. The codes indicate the town, sector, and even the individual postman's beat, which means that there can be hundreds of postcodes for some towns. Codes for London begin with letters that indicate which geographical section of the city the address is located in (e.g., SW means southwest, EC means east central). Main post offices and reference libraries have postcode directories available.

The environment

Landscape   The English countryside is hard to beat for sheer compact diversity and loveliness. One of the great pleasures of traveling around England lies in watching one kind of landscape melt into a different kind within a very short distance.

Much of the southern and midland countryside has a cozy, tamed feel to it. Most of the land is in use, with attractively irregular fields that are edged by hedgerows, trees, or stacked-stone walls which divide the rolling land. Parts of the north and far southwest where the land is hillier, the soil poorer, and the population less dense provide more rugged areas where you can commune with nature in near solitude. The entire country seems green year-round.

Uplands   For those who like mountain scenery, there are a few low mountain ranges in the north of England. The highest peak is Scafell Pike in the Lake District at 978 meters (3210 feet). The tree line in England lies at only 610 meters (2000 feet), so the taller mountains are bare and rugged. A ridge of hills called the Pennines, also known as the 'backbone of England,' runs from the Scottish border down to the center of England. Many other areas of the country have high, rolling hills.

In parts of the north, hills are called *fells*, and fell walking is a popular pastime. The south includes many low, rounded, grass-covered chalk ridges known as *downs*. The valleys that lie between the mountains and the hills are called *dales* in some northern areas and *coombes* in the southwest.

Moors can be found in various parts of the country. These are high, treeless, wind-swept areas covered with very low shrubs and heather. They can be delightful romantic and colorful spots in the summer and autumn, but are bleak, cold, and uncomfortable in the winter. *Heathland* is sandy, low, open land covered with heather (which comes out in purple blooms in the autumn) and gorse (a prickly evergreen shrub with yellow flowers).

Large forests and small woodlands (very small ones   *Forests* are called *copses*) are scattered about the country, but only a very low percentage of the land is now forested. The term *plantation* refers to an area planted with trees, usually conifers, and not to a cotton farm manned by slaves.

Low-lying areas such as peat bogs, marshland, and   *Lowlands* *fens* still exist but are receding due to the draining of the land by farmers. Those that are left are wonderful for birdwatching. The Fens in East Anglia and the Somerset Levels are known for being incredibly flat even by English standards.

Besides the mighty Thames (pronounced 'temz'),   *Water* other major rivers, canals, and hundreds of smaller rivers and streams (in some places called *becks*) cut through the countryside. Small lakes dot parts of the north. The lengthy coastline includes an incredible variety of features: chalk cliffs and rocky ridges plunging down to the sea; beaches and coves of sand, pebble, or shale; and estuaries teeming with birds.

England contains seven national parks, all of which   **Parks** are free to visit. England also boasts forest parks, areas of outstanding natural beauty, and numerous small countryside parks and nature reserves. All of these have been established to help preserve what is left of the dwindling countryside. Considering that England has a population of over 48 million in an area of less than one-quarter the size of France, there is a surprising amount of open space left. This may be due to the fact the most cities and towns are very compact.

Many villages are centered on a village green. In larger urban centers, parks and gardens of various sizes give the residents something enjoyable to look at. They often include benches, formal gardens, and perhaps a bandstand, but may not supply playground equipment. The major parks in London, which are very large, are a real joy to visit after a busy day on the noisy streets.

Surrounding major urban areas are *green belts*, areas of countryside which, thankfully, have been set aside so that no building development can blight the scenery. These have kept urban sprawl in check to some degree and help city dwellers feel that they aren't too far from the country.

Cities and towns
Large English cities are very different from their U.S. counterparts. Many have tall buildings, but except in London, you won't see many skyscrapers. Cities tend to have well-defined centers that are lively and bustling and still residential, as is the case in many European countries, although there is now some movement of shops to outlying malls. The larger cities tend to be industrial and can't really be considered beautiful, but many smaller ones are very pleasant. Some cities have an untidy look to them nowadays, partly because of cut-backs in street cleaning and partly because most trash-baskets don't have lids on them, so the wind blows the paper out. But a majority are also attractive and of considerable historical interest.

One striking feature of English cities and towns is the cramped look of their rows and rows of nearly identical terraced houses with their legions of chimney pots. To tell one house from another in these anonymous rows, the residents paint their window frames and doors in distinctive and often rather loud (some might say tasteless) colors, which may not be in harmony with neighboring houses. Very few houses are made of wood. Timber is a limited resource in England, and materials such as brick, sandstone, granite, flint, and stone are more easily available, depending on what is most prevalent in the particular area; it can be fascinating to see the changes in materials as you drive from one area to another. Sometimes one material is used for most of the house and a different color or type of material used around the windows and edges for decoration. Decorative plasterwork called *pargetting* appears on some houses in the southeast.

Since there is little garden space in many cities and towns, marginal areas are often set aside for garden allotments, which can be rented from the local council. These patchworks of small plots and sheds liven up what would otherwise be derelict areas near train tracks and roadsides.

Villages

Villages can be very small indeed, consisting sometimes of only a church, pub, general store-cum-post office, and a few old houses. Thriving village communities provide visitors with glimpses of English life and values that won't easily be found elsewhere. Lack of public transportation into larger towns, not enough housing for younger people, and few jobs are leading some rural villages down the road to extinction, although in the prosperous south-east most villages have expanded enormously over the last forty years.

Regions and their features

One distinction that you must get straight right from the start is that the terms *England* and *Britain* do not refer to the same entity. Many tourists insult the Scots and Welsh by talking about England when they really mean Britain. *Britain* (or Great Britain – a reference to size, not status) is made up of England, Scotland, and the principality of Wales. Scotland was united with England in 1603. It has some degree of local autonomy, but in many respects has less than the German states, for instance. Wales has been politically dominated by England since 1535. It has very little say in its governmental affairs, yet retains a strong cultural identity.

The term *United Kingdom* (U.K.) refers to Britain and Northern Ireland. All four countries of the U.K. are represented in the British Parliament. The *British Isles* include all the islands in the area: Great Britain, Ireland, the Isle of Man (a Crown dependency lying between northern England and Ireland), and the Channel Islands (also a Crown dependency, lying very near to France).

England and Wales are divided into counties of various sizes, while Scotland is divided into regions. However, these administrative divisions don't always coincide with the larger or more natural regions that people commonly refer to. The following regional terms are often used in the media and in general; many of the boundaries are impressionistic rather than clear-cut.

England's counties and major towns

Those counties that border on London. These tend to *Home* be wealthy, suburban, and fashionably rural areas. *Counties* Natural features in this area include the Chiltern hills to the northwest, the North Downs to the southeast, lovely heathlands in Surrey, woodland and orchards in Kent, and, of course, the river Thames.

London, the eastern Home Counties, and East and *Southeast* West Sussex. This area takes in the South Downs and some lovely and popular beaches on the south coast.

Either the southern half of England or the south- *South* central coast. Besides the overpopular coastal areas and the Isle of Wight (which has rolling countryside typical of southern England), the south includes the New Forest, which is 900 years old.

Mainly the peninsula comprising Cornwall, Devon, *Southwest* and Somerset. This is largely a rural area with a varied and spectacular coast (including surfing spots), open moorland (Dartmoor and Exmoor), and ranges of low hills (the Mendips and Quantocks).

The Southwest plus those areas to the west of *West Country* Winchester and north almost to Birmingham. Again, this is a rural, agricultural area. Its natural features include Salisbury Plain, the beautiful Cotswold hills, the many lovely hills and valleys along the Welsh border, and the Forest of Dean.

The thumb of land sticking into the North Sea to the *East Anglia* northeast of London. It includes Norfolk, Suffolk, and some of Cambridgeshire and Essex. This area is thought to be very flat by English standards, espe- cially the Fens. It has a variety of coastal scenery and a network of inland waterways known as the Broads.

Extends from Oxford up to Cheshire and Lincoln- *Midlands* shire and divides into the East and West Midlands. It is the industrial heartland of England. (The heavily industrial part north of Birmingham goes by the unappealing name of the Black Country.) The area is quite beautiful in places, however, with rolling hills, woodland (including Sherwood Forest), and many rivers. Stratford-upon-Avon, Shakespeare's birthplace, is also in the Midlands.

Peak District   A lovely area of open hills (without actual peaks, despite the name), rivers, and valleys, lying between Sheffield and Manchester.

The North   From Liverpool and Sheffield northward. Many parts are industrial, but outside the cities you can readily find moorland, dales (Yorkshire's are famous), woodlands, and varied coasts with nice beaches.

Lake District   In Cumbria, in the northwest of England. This is a popular holiday area consisting of low mountains, valleys, beautiful lakes, and lovely beaches.

Northeast   Mainly Durham and Northumberland. This area boasts moorland, thick forests, and beautiful coasts, as well as industry and mines. The remains of Hadrian's Wall run across the region, looking like a natural ridge in places. A range of hills called the Cheviots straddles the borders of Northumberland and Scotland.

River regions   A few major rivers lend their names to the areas lining their banks. *Merseyside* is the region around the river Mersey, including Liverpool; *Teesside* is on the east coast, around Middlesbrough; *Humberside*, also on the east coast, is around Hull; and *Tyneside* centers on Newcastle, in the far northeast.

Getting around

The whole of Great Britain is roughly the same size as the U.S. state of Utah, or Honshu (Japan's largest island), or the Australian province of Victoria. Its relatively small size makes it ideal for the traveler. By North American or Australian standards, nothing is very far away. The distance from John o'Groats (a place, not a person, in the far northeast of Scotland) to the appropriately named Land's End (at the southwest tip of England) is only about 850 miles (1368 kilometers) by road. Even at the widest part of the country, you are seldom more than 75 miles (120 kilometers) from the sea.

From London it is easy to take day trips by car, bus, or train to many interesting places, such as Bath, Stonehenge, the Isle of Wight, Canterbury, Oxford, Cambridge, Stratford-upon-Avon, and Norwich. By fast train (see 'By train' below) you can even make day trips to Cardiff, York, Manchester, Lincoln, and Chester. Coach companies in provincial towns also run day-trips to shopping centers and places of interest throughout the country, and for the intrepid there are 'mystery tours' – generally excursions to the nearest seaside town.

Most urban areas of England are fairly easy to get to and around in without having to rely on a car. However, you will have to be prepared to bend your schedule to that of public transportation. Of course, if you really want to get away from everyone, you'll have to use private transportation.

By air

Many major cities and towns in Britain are served by domestic airlines. This is convenient if you are short on time, but flying within the country is expensive. There are also air services to the larger off-shore islands, such as the Channel Islands, the Isles of

Scilly, the Isle of Man, the Outer Hebrides, and the Orkney and Shetland Islands.

British Airways, until recently state-owned, but now a privatized airline, bases its domestic flights to and from London at Terminal 1 of Heathrow Airport. A particularly useful service that BA offers is the no-reservation shuttle. The shuttle flights go directly to Edinburgh, Glasgow, Manchester, and Belfast, leaving every hour or two on weekdays. British Caledonian Airways also offers some shuttle services. Other domestic airlines base their London flights at Gatwick Airport and offer flights to a variety of regional airports.

By train Train travel is popular in Britain, as it is in most of Europe. Going by train can be an enjoyable way to see a good deal of the countryside as well as being time-saving and relaxing. The British Rail network is extensive, with frequent services on major routes. Trains usually run on time, although equipment failure, sudden local strikes or staff shortages occasionally disrupt services. Trains generally aren't as frequent on Sundays and holidays, and they can be much slower at those times, since that is when track maintenance is carried out. There are no trains on Christmas or Boxing Day (December 25 and 26).

The Intercity 125 trains, so called because they have a maximum speed of 125 mph, are mainly used on routes from London to the west and north. Other main-line trains are diesel-powered or electric and also travel at a fast pace. Branch-line train trips should be considered opportunities to enjoy the scenery at a leisurely pace.

Fares The fare structure may be subject to some change, but basically there are two sorts of ticket: standard (you can go on any train; return tickets are valid for three months), and the cheaper Saver (you can only use off-peak trains to and from London; return tickets are valid for one month). Foreign visitors can buy a British Rail Card, which, like the Eurail pass, entitles you to unlimited travel for a specified number of weeks, but these must be bought (from your travel agent) *before* coming to Britain. Other bargains include regional rail passes, half-price student discounts (when a valid student card is shown), family rail cards, and cheaper fares for children (free for those under five, although they have to sit on someone's lap if necessary; half-price for those under sixteen). It pays to ask if there are any special cheap fares, as new ones are introduced from time to time. First-class fares are roughly one and a half times second-class fares, and singles (one-way fares) cost much more than half of the return (round-trip) fare.

You can buy train tickets from many travel agents, such as Thomas Cook, as well as at train stations. Credit cards are accepted for payment at train stations. You can also buy a ticket on the train, but you'll have to pay the more expensive standard fare.

Tickets

Ticket collectors may ask to see your ticket more than once on a trip if there are many stops, so keep it on hand. You may also have to show your ticket before entering or when leaving the station platform. At such stations, if you want to see someone off at the train window, you have to buy a platform ticket for a few pence. Other stations are called 'open stations'.

Reservations

Trains can be very crowded in the summer, on holiday weekends, and during peak commuter hours. If you are unlucky at such times, you may end up standing on the train. If traveling then, it is a very good idea to get to the station early (you may have to wait in ticket queues a long time, especially in London), or to reserve a seat (up to two hours ahead of time) for a small fee so that you won't have to stand. You cannot reserve a seat over the telephone, which is just as well since British Rail is notorious for taking ages to answer its phones (it has a call-stacking system; if you wait patiently you will be answered!) You should reserve a seat on any long-distance train in the summer, especially on those going to Scotland or the southwest of England; in fact, reservations are required at certain times on these trains. Fridays, Saturday mornings, and Sundays are the most difficult days for getting seats.

If you want a sleeping berth on an overnight train, you must reserve one. With a second-class ticket you get a bed in a two-berth cabin, and with a first-class ticket, a single-berth cabin. Sleeping accommodation is generally comfortable. The cabins include a wash-basin, hot and cold water, towels, and soap; you are even brought tea or coffee in the morning. Some cheaper night trains to Scotland do not have berths but do have adjustable seats and a video lounge.

Stations   London has more than a dozen train stations that serve particular routes: Waterloo and Victoria stations for the south and southeast; Paddington Station for the west of England and south Wales; Euston and St. Pancras stations for the Midlands, the northwest, and north Wales; King's Cross Station for the northeast; and Liverpool Street Station for the east. If you don't know or can't remember which station you need and don't have access to a train schedule, ask a taxi driver. All the stations are connected by the Underground system (see pp. 60–2), so it isn't hard to go from one to another if you don't have too much luggage. If you do need to cross London to change stations, your British Rail ticket will be valid on the Underground.

Some small stations in rural Scotland and Wales are 'request stops,' which means that you have to wave the train down in order to get on and tell the guard (conductor) where you want to get off.

Most English train stations are fairly old and a bit rundown, but British Rail is trying to spruce them up. They can be very cold, damp, and drafty in the winter. Toilets are generally clean, but not always free of charge (you need the right coins to open the doors). Women's toilets are often found through the ladies' waiting room.

The larger stations have stalls that sell newspapers, magazines, postcards, some books, cigarettes, candy, snack food, and flowers; the largest ones may also have shops that sell gifts, travel goods, and liquor, as well as a barber, a restaurant, a bar, a tourist information desk, and a bureau de change. Luggage trolleys may be available on the platforms.

Train timetables (schedules) are posted clearly on large boards at main-line stations. Note that they use the twenty-four-hour clock, so that, for example 1:55 p.m. is 13.55, 8:05 p.m. is 20.05, and midnight is 24.00. You can also phone British Rail for scheduling information; in some cases you can get tape-recorded timetables for popular routes. Announcements over the loudspeakers may be difficult to understand, and the guards (conductors) are not necessarily much easier to understand if you aren't acquainted with the local accent (see the chapter on 'Understanding the Natives (and Being Understood)'). Larger stations carry impending departures and arrivals on monitors or display boards.

An intriguing sight at many stations is that of boys and men wandering the platforms with small notebooks, scribbling away as the trains go by. They are not sketching the trains, or even counting them; they are writing down the serial number of each train's engine. This thrilling hobby is known as train spotting. In the days of steam engines, when each looked different, this probably was an interesting pastime. Now, however, it is difficult to see the attraction. Perhaps this is best put down to English eccentricity.

Train cars

Newer trains have automatic doors between the carriages (cars), and extra luggage racks at the ends of each car as well as overhead and between the backs of seats. Not-so-new cars use sliding doors with very stiff springs, and provide space for luggage only between and above seats. Seats are usually arranged in groups of four around a small table. Toilets are located at the ends of every car; water is operated by a foot pedal and is for washing only, not for drinking. There may be a trash bin by the toilet, but usually the rubbish just piles up on the tables until a porter clears it away near the end of the trip.

Old carriages, which are used mainly on the small branch lines, have nice woodwork and are often divided into compartments without tables that seat eight. Others have odd seating configurations, such as room for two and a half people on one seat and one and a half on the other side of the aisle!

There are smoking and nonsmoking sections on the trains (look for red and white stickers on the windows that indicate the no-smoking areas). However, some trains have only a partial barrier between the sections, which is annoyingly ineffective against smoke. Newer long-distance trains have entire cars designated as smoking or nonsmoking, a much better system.

First-class carriages are roomier than the others and often have the advantage of being closer to the dining car. They are also usually much emptier.

Handles for the train doors are located only on the outside of the train. When you want to get off the train, you have to push the window down, lean out, and hope that your arm is long enough to reach the handle.

Food　Food services of various sorts are available on many routes – the type of service will be indicated on the train schedule (restaurant car, or buffet car with hot snacks, or cold snack bar). However, be prepared for catering services to be unexpectedly canceled, which is often announced only after the train has pulled out of the station! Food services are almost nonexistent on Sunday trains.

British Rail food has improved lately. The restaurant meals are on the expensive side, but you do get good waiter service, a linen tablecloth, and real silverware. Besides adding a touch of elegance to a train journey, eating in the dining car allows you to travel in a first-class compartment with a second-class ticket (at least while you dine). At lunch and dinner, there is a choice of main dishes, and some of the vegetables are fresh, as are the salads. Afternoon tea includes a plentiful amount of tea and goodies. Breakfasts are the full-blown affairs (see p. 20).

You can buy alcoholic drinks on the train as well as tea, coffee, hot chocolate, and some soft drinks. If you are not used to drinking on a train, remember to lift your cup or glass off the table when pouring something into it, so a sudden jolt doesn't direct it to your lap.

Buffet cars have limited offerings, usually just sandwiches, potato crisps (potato chips), and various cakes, tarts, and sweets. Those that serve hot snacks offer toasted sandwiches, hamburgers, and the like. Not all buffet cars have seats and tables. On some routes, a trolley with drinks and snacks is wheeled through the train.

Automobiles

British Rail operates a Motorail service on certain routes, which permits you to put your car on the train (often overnight) and saves you the strain of driving. These routes include: London to Penzance (in the far southwest); London to Carlisle (in the northwest); London to various places in Scotland; Bristol (in the southwest) to Edinburgh; and Crewe (in the west) to Inverness. You must book in advance.

If you want to have a rental car waiting for you at your destination, you can book one through the Rail Drive (Godfrey Davis) service at major train stations.

Bicycles

Bicycles can be taken on many trains, but are not allowed on trains going into or out of London during peak commuter hours. They are usually carried free of charge on weekends, but there may be a substantial charge on intercity trains during the week. Bicycles are kept in the guard's van (the carriage where the guard and the mail ride, normally near the end of the train).

Pets

Don't be surprised if a person sitting near you on the train has a dog on his or her lap or underfoot – small, well-behaved pets are allowed in the passenger compartments (but not in the dining or sleeping cars). Dogs have to pay one-half the second-class fare.

Steam trains

Train enthusiasts will be delighted by the number of old steam trains still in operation on special lines. Most of these are privately owned and operated, and are usually located in very scenic areas around the country. Some are run only in the summer.

By bus
Long-distance

Intercity express buses are known as coaches. Both the state-run National Express and private coach *buses* companies compete for business, offering relatively inexpensive fares (often half the price of train fares) and fairly frequent services. National Express sells bus passes that operate much like rail passes.

Express-coach journeys can be very fast (in fact some companies have schedules that seem to force the drivers to break the speed limits). Newer coaches may be air-conditioned, but there are still a lot that don't have toilets on board. On the longer, popular routes you may be treated to some food and drink, sit in reclining seats, and even be able to watch videos; some of these coaches are double-decker ones, allowing you a wonderful view of the scenery. Smoking sections are usually provided at the rear of the coaches.

The main station in London for express coaches is Victoria Coach Station, which is about one-third of a mile from Victoria Underground station.

Bus tours Many private coach companies offer 'package tours' to major cities and other tourist attractions; the price may include one or two nights' accommodation in a guest house or hotel. Such tours can be very good value for money. Find out before you book if the coach has toilets and air-conditioning.

Rural buses Rural bus service is infrequent and getting worse. Some villages have only one bus per week into the nearest town of any size, which causes difficulties for the inhabitants and tourists alike. In some remote areas, people use the Mail Bus, a postal van seating a small number of people which stops everywhere along the mail route. This may be slow traveling, but it does give you a chance to talk with local people.

Urban buses Most visitors to England are very keen to ride on the top of a double-decker bus. In London, you can just hop on one of the special sightseeing buses that go around to the major tourist attractions. In other places, you may have to satisfy your urge on a normal bus. And that means you have to know which bus goes where at what time.

It is not always easy to get a bus schedule for a

particular area: comprehensive schedules aren't provided on each bus, and you may have to go to the
town's central station to get one. In London, major
Underground stations have bus schedules at the ticket
booths. Some bus stops post the schedule for that
particular route, but there may not be a map of the
route.

One important part of taking a bus is queuing up at
the bus stop. (It has been said that England is the only
place where you can see one person forming a queue.)
It is particularly bad manners to 'jump the queue' or
even just to lounge around in a disorderly fashion at
the stop. You must also make sure that you queue up
in the correct direction from the bus stop sign (it
usually says 'queue this side' if this isn't obvious).
There may be more than one bus using the same stop,
so make sure you join the right queue and look for
the bus number on the front of the bus. Some bus
stops are labeled 'request stop,' which means that the
bus will stop only if you signal it by sticking out your
hand. At a multi-bus stop, you should step back or
shake your head 'no' if the bus coming isn't the one
you want.

London buses are notorious for 'hunting in packs':
you wait a long time for the bus, then three will show
up at once. Try not to get too frustrated by this – use
the opportunity to strike up a conversation with a
fellow-sufferer.

Avoid taking a bus at peak commuter times and
before and after school (schoolchildren use the public
buses). Saturday afternoons are also bad times for
finding a seat.

Fares vary widely from place to place and are
usually based on the distance traveled rather than a
flat rate. Have plenty of coins with you, as large notes
aren't appreciated. In some places (notably Birmingham) you must have the exact fare, although there is
no way of knowing what it will be. If you don't want
to worry about having enough change for each bus,
you can buy a bus pass. London Transport sells cheap
passes for unlimited travel on both the buses and the
Underground that are valid for a specified period –
even for just one day. Other places sell discount bus

passes, but these are often for a minimum of one month.

On most buses, you tell the driver your destination (e.g., 'one for Piccadilly Circus'), pay the appropriate fare, and take a receipt from the ticket machine. Keep your receipt until you get off the bus, as ticket inspectors sometimes come around. Other buses have conductors who collect the fare from you after you are seated. If you aren't sure when to get off the bus, ask the driver or conductor to announce your stop. Otherwise, press the button or ceiling strip to ring the bell in good time for the bus to halt at your stop.

Usually you get on the bus at the front and off at the door in the middle, although older buses have an open back stairway where you can get on or off (people sometimes make daring leaps from these while the bus is moving!). Make sure you sit down or grab on to a rail as soon as you can, because the driver may start up as soon as all passengers are on, whether or not they are seated.

The upper deck of the bus is the only place where smoking is permitted. The upper deck also gives you the best view, as well as the most exciting ride. It can be quite bumpy and even a little scary sitting at the front on the top – it looks as if you are going to squash the car in front of the bus or get entangled in the trees. If you do sit on the top deck, make sure you are downstairs by the time the bus stops at your destination so that you don't keep everyone waiting.

Most buses provide a small storage space near the front where you can put large items such as luggage, folding push chairs (baby strollers), shopping bags, etc.

London and some other large urban areas run express suburban commuter buses. These can be a quick and inexpensive way to get out of the congestion of the city and into outlying country areas.

The Underground   The London Underground system – commonly called the Tube – is an extensive network of underground trains serving inner London and its suburbs. (Note that if you ask for the 'subway,' you will be directed to a pedestrian tunnel under a road, not to the Tube.) Trains are frequent on most of the ten lines, with service starting at about 5:30 a.m. and ending around midnight. Sunday service isn't as frequent as during the week and doesn't begin until 7:30 a.m.

The Underground is easier (and safer) to use than you might first think. Large color-coded maps of the network are prominently displayed at all stations, and people are usually helpful if you can't figure out how to get where you want to go. Electronic travel planners are available at a few stations: you just push the button for your destination and the route appears on a screen. Free maps of the system are available from the inquiry offices at the stations and appear in most guidebooks and on London street maps.

Considering that the London Underground was the first of its kind, it is in very good shape. The stations have seen better days, but many are now being renovated. However, they tend to be drafty and cold in the winter and hot and sticky in the summer. Most have a small kiosk (stand) that sells newspapers, candy, and cigarettes, and larger ones may have several rows of shops leading to the platforms. There are few public toilets at stations.

Fares depend on the distance traveled, with children going for half price. You can transfer from one Underground line to another with the same ticket. Tickets can be bought either at a counter or from coin-operated machines that list the destinations for that fare. You may need to show your ticket before heading for the platform; at some stations there are automatic turnstiles into which you insert your ticket to get through (don't forget to retrieve it on the top of the turnstile!). Keep you ticket until the end of your journey because you must hand it over when you leave. Remember that you can buy a London Transport combined pass that allows you unlimited travel on the Tube and the buses for a specified period.

You will need to know both the name of the line and the direction the train you want is headed (e.g., Central Line eastbound or westbound); there are maps and signs that will direct you to the proper platform. When the train arrives, check on the front or on the indicator board, if there is one, to make sure the final destination is that of the train you want – some lines divide, and some trains do not go all the way to the end of the line. When changing lines, look carefully on the platform for signs for the line and direction that you want; you may have to use stairs or escalators to get to another platform.

Most Tube trains have fully automatic doors. On a few, however, you have to push a large button to open the door. The train cars are fairly clean and comfortable when not crowded (that is, not during peak commuter hours or on Saturday afternoons). Maps of the train's particular route are displayed above the doors and windows of the car so that you'll know when your stop is coming up. Non-smokers will be delighted to know that there is no smoking on the trains or on the platforms.

London isn't the only English city with an underground system. Liverpool has one, and Tyneside has a light rapid transit system.

By taxi   Except in London, taxis don't usually cruise the streets looking for business. You can hail a taxi that has its 'For Hire' sign lit, but in most cases outside London you will have to locate a taxi rank or phone for a taxi. Taxi ranks are often situated at train stations and near busy tourist spots, including high-class hotels, but don't tend to be near shopping areas. When waiting at a taxi rank, you are expected to form an orderly queue.

London taxis are distinctive large, squarish, black cars. The driver is separated from the passengers by a clear panel, and only the luggage is allowed to ride in the front with the driver. Outside of London, most taxis are just ordinary cars with a taxi sign on the roof. Fares should be listed inside the taxi, and there should be a meter in view – if not, don't get in. Drivers expect a 10 percent tip on top of the fare. Almost all drivers will help you with you luggage.

London taxi drivers tend to be friendly and can cope with the most horrendous traffic. They have an amazing knowledge of where every street in London is. This is because they have to pass a very difficult test on getting around the city, which takes two years to train for (known as 'doing the knowledge').

Some taxis can be hired for short or long sightseeing tours, an expensive way of seeing the sights, but more relaxing and personal.

By water

Britain has over 2000 miles of navigable canals and rivers. You can travel through much of the country at a leisurely pace by hiring a boat (see p. 21); it is a very good way to view the scenery and wildlife that can't be seen from the road. You can also take short sightseeing tours by boat on various rivers (such as the Thames) and lakes. Some sightseeing boats can be taken just for one-way travel – a sort of water-taxi service.

Ferries

Regular year-round ferry service to all the major islands off Britain is available. Some ferries, however, do not take cars. At the height of the season, you should make a booking at a travel agent for the longer ferry journeys.

By bicycle

The bicycle is a common form of transportation in England. People of all ages and walks of life ride bicycles to work, to the shops, and generally just to get around. In spite of the volume of bicycle use, however, there is woefully inadequate provision for cyclists, particularly in the cites. Few separate bicycle paths exist in urban areas, although bicycles are allowed to use some bus lanes. And narrow streets congested with traffic can make city cycling less than pleasurable. There never seem to be enough bicycle racks at popular locations.

Cycling in the countryside, on the other hand, can be an enjoyable and inexpensive way to see the delights of rural England. The going isn't too difficult, although the low rolling hills may be more demanding than they look. In any case, you don't have to set out on a long bicycle ride to get somewhere, as villages tend to be only a short distance apart. But do be careful when riding on narrow, twisty country lanes bordered by hedges because it is not easy for cars or lorries (trucks) to see you on the road.

Bicycle rental shops can be found in London and in most tourist and university areas. You have a choice of number of gears on the bike you rent, and can usually rent either by the day or by the week.

By foot Ramblers (walkers and hikers) will find England a marvelous place to get around in on foot. An extensive network of public footpaths runs throughout the country. Most of these dirt paths represent old rights-of-way: some are Iron Age or Roman paths, some are old cattle-droving ways, others are well-known long-distance scenic paths, while others simply connect villages or farms or skirt rivers and hills. Paths are well marked and can be found on detailed Ordnance Survey maps (see below, pp. 66–7). One of the fringe benefits of country walks is that you can usually end up at a country pub (also marked on the maps).

Farmers who have public footpaths running along or through their property are obliged by law to keep the paths open and to keep stiles over fences in good repair. However, they sometimes put a bull in the field to discourage ramblers. Walkers should always stick to the paths and not venture into fields or meadows.

Walking is also one of the best ways to explore the interesting nooks and crannies of the cities and towns. On foot it is possible to discover architectural delights, interesting little shops, and peaceful corners that you could easily miss from a car or bus. Some cities, towns, and universities offer free guided walking tours – ask at the Tourist Office.

Americans will find the lack of street violence – or even fear of it - refreshing. In town centres and suburban areas it is perfectly normal for women to walk around alone in the evening. Of course, there are some areas where you are less secure; if possible avoid lonely underpasses late at night if you're alone.

Crossing When crossing a street, remember that traffic will be
streets   coming first from your right. At some crossing places

on divided streets there will be a message on the road to 'Look Right' or 'Look Left.'

You will encounter two types of pedestrian crossing in England: the 'zebra' crossing and the 'pelican' crossing. The first is a black-and-white-striped path across the road, with flashing yellow globes stuck on poles at either side. Cars must stop for you when you are on a zebra crossing (but don't just leap out – give drivers a chance to see you). In London, drivers try to ignore pedestrians who are perched at the edge of a crossing hoping that the cars will stop. The pelican crossing is safer to use because it is controlled by a traffic light. You simply push the button next to the crossing and wait for the green man to light up on the sign; this is accompanied by a bleeping sound for blind people. When the green man starts flashing, that means the light is about to change back to red.

City layouts

If you look at a map of almost any English city or town, you can easily see that it grew with a will of its own. Twisting lanes and bending roads stop and start and come together at strange angles. It is difficult to take a walk around the block in most cities, as there is really no such entity. You can easily get turned around in the wrong direction in most urban areas if you don't have a map with you. Even English people carry maps of London when they enter that maze.

Street names seem to change by whim – you merely have to go up a hill, around a slight bend, or across an intersection to find that the name has become something else. Street names themselves can keep you amused as you wander around: Carbuncle Passage, Lower Goat Lane, Rampant Horse Street, and Zinzan Street are all real names. It is important to note whether the street name ends in *Road*, *Avenue*, etc., since the main name may appear more than once in a city.

Street name signs are generally plentiful, although main road names aren't signposted at every minor intersection. Signs are sometimes difficult to spot; many are placed on the sides of buildings, about one story above the ground, but others may be on low walls or on posts just a few feet off the ground. House numbers tend to run with odd numbers on one side of the street and evens on the other, but sometimes they progress up one side of the road and down the other.

London   London, the largest city in Europe, is a conglomerate of different neighborhoods, boroughs, and villages, all of which have their own personalities. Traditional guidebooks will tell you which areas are fashionable, which are good for shopping or eating, etc. Many people are confused by the term *the City*, which does *not* refer to London as a whole but rather to the banking and commercial area of London.

Take a good map with you when you venture into London because you will definitely need it. (An excellent map book that details all the streets of London is *London A-Z*, pronounced 'ay to zed,' which is available in bookshops, newsagents and many other shops.) If you do get lost, the locals are usually happy to give you directions if you ask politely. However, they may know only their patch of London, and in the summer it can be difficult to find a Londoner anyway. Policemen are always good for giving directions and are quite used to being asked for them.

Maps   Whether you are exploring England by car, bicycle, or foot, a good set of maps is indispensable. Few journeys are straightforward – there is always a choice of ways to get from one place to another, depending on what kind of roads or countryside appeal to you. There are many good series of maps, but the Ordnance Survey maps, obtainable at many bookstores and tourist shops, are probably the easiest to follow and include a good range of information.

If you are just interested in driving to major cities and towns on the main roads, then the Ordnance Survey Routeplanner map, which shows all of Britain, will be adequate. The Route Master series is best for touring by car. It consists of nine maps that show almost all roads, major places of interest, and height contours. If you want to explore a particular area in detail, then the Landranger series of 204 area maps is a must. These maps show all roads (no matter how small), service areas, parking places, footpaths, topographical features (height contours, marshes, forests, etc), scenic viewpoints, ancient monuments and sites, pubs, churches, public toilets, telephone boxes, youth hostels, farms, buildings, and much more. You really can't get lost if you have one of these maps, unless you're just one of those people who can't read maps.

For walkers and climbers, there are even more detailed Ordnance maps that show rights of way, field boundaries, and very detailed topographic features such as loose rock, rough grassland, etc. You can also buy special tourist maps for the National Park areas and for Greater London, which include information about places of interest, camping sites, viewpoints, parking, etc. Special archaeological and historical maps are also available.

Driving

Everyone knows that the British (and most of their former colonists) drive on the wrong side of the road. Don't let that put you off driving in England, though – it isn't that difficult to get used to driving on the left. But don't assume that the *only* difference about driving in England lies in keeping to the 'other' side of the road. There are several other important ways in which the English rules of the road differ from those in other countries (see below).

Conditions The English are not as polite behind the wheel as you might expect. Many become aggressive, nipping in and out of traffic in their little cars, often without signaling their intentions. On two-lane roads, drivers of slower vehicles sometimes stubbornly refuse to pull off to let other traffic go by. Some don't turn on their headlights until absolutely necessary. But they seldom use their car horns in anger.

In general, road conditions are fairly good year-round. In the winter, however, there may be snow on the hills or in deep country lanes, icy roads after dark, and fog in low-lying areas. When roads get slippery, they are often 'gritted.' If there is a lot of snow, minor roads can be blocked for hours or days, as there isn't an adequate amount of snow-removal equipment around.

Driving in England at other times can be far from relaxing. There are few straight roads, and many main routes include sections with only two lanes, which makes for very slow going if you get stuck behind a lorry (truck) or farm vehicle. Traffic is dense in urban areas at peak times (8 to 9:30 a.m., 12:30 to 2 p.m., and 4:30 to 6:30 p.m.) and on weekends. But if you get into the quieter parts of the countryside, you may seldom meet another vehicle.

You must be seventeen to drive a car in England and sixteen to drive a moped. Visitors can drive for up to twelve months on a valid license from another country. Foreign residents are supposed either to take a driving test after three months or get a provisional license. It is not easy to pass a British driving test, which involves about 20 minutes of driving and maneuvering. People who haven't passed the test must display a red L plate (for 'learner') on the car so that other road users will know to beware and be patient. You should also beware of old men wearing caps while they drive – they almost always drive too slowly.

Cars are generally on the smaller end of the scale – Cadillacs look like tanks next to most British and European cars. Most have four-cylinder engines, and the engine size is given in liters. Terms for car types include:

saloon:	4-door, sedan
coupé:	2-door
estate:	station wagon
dormobile:	van with sleeping accommodation
hatchback:	saloon with single large rear door for luggage

Some peculiar-looking vehicles can be found on English roads. One odd type is the three-wheeled car (only one wheel at the front), some of which are adapted for disabled drivers. These can go at normal speeds, even if they look a bit unstable. Another strange vehicle is the very slow, electrically powered milk 'float,' a van with open sides and crates of milk bottles stacked dangerously inside. Yet another is the 'half-timbered' old Mini estate car, which actually has wooden beams supporting the back.

You can tell how old a car is by the number plate, which is permanently attached to the car. A single letter at one end of the plate indicates the year that the car was registered. For example, the letter *A* at the front stands for 1983–84, while *A* at the end is for

1963; *X* at the end is for 1981–82, and *M* at the end is for 1974. The letters I, O, Q, U, and Z aren't used.

The English aren't too keen on bumper stickers, although these are on the increase. The current rage is to put a plastic strip across the top of the front window with the owners' first names on it (e.g., 'Mike and Kathy,' with the man's name always on the driver's side of the car).

Cars
Bringing yours

If you are bringing your own car to England, be sure to also have your car registration papers, your driver's license, and at least third-party insurance. You must display a nationality sticker on the back of the car. Don't forget to adjust your headlights so that the beam angles to the left. And remember, the larger your car or camper is, the more difficult it will be to drive along the narrow country lanes and to park on congested city streets.

Rentals

There are many car hire (rental) firms in England. You can arrange fly-drive or rail-drive package trips, which ensure that a car will be waiting for you when you arrive in the country. If you plan on renting a car during the peak holiday times, make reservations well in advance. The cost of insurance will usually be included; make sure you *are* covered.

The majority of rental cars have manual transmissions. If you are anxious about driving on the right-hand side of the car (and thus shifting the gears with your left hand), then you will probably be more comfortable and safer renting an automatic. Most automatics have the gears on the floor, not on the steering column, so don't panic and think you've been given a manual shift.

Expenses

Cars are expensive to run in England. The purchase price can be up to twice what it is in America and is often up to 30 percent more than the European equivalent. The yearly road tax (the car licensing system) is also costly – about £100 a year now. (When you pay the tax (at a post office), for either six or twelve months, you get a paper disc to put in the car window.) After a car is three years old, you must pay

to have a comprehensive MOT (Ministry of Transport) test done at a garage every year to ensure that
the car is in safe working order. And petrol (gas) is
very expensive, in spite of North Sea oil. Perhaps all
this explains why only about half of all British
households own a car.

The first thing you should do before driving in
England is to study a copy of *The Highway Code*,
which outlines the rules of the road and shows signs
and road markings. This can be bought very cheaply
(for about 35p) at many book stores. You can also get
copies from the British Tourist Authority and the
various Automobile Associations. It is very irres-
ponsible to drive in any foreign country without
knowing the rules of the road; *don't* assume you'll be
able to figure them out as you go.

Driving preliminaries

Seat belts must be worn by people in the front of
the car, and you can be fined for not doing so.
Motorcyclists and scooter drivers must wear an
approved type of safety helmet.

Do not drive if you have been drinking. Penalties
can be stiff, and if you are not in full control of your
vehicle you can be prosecuted whether or not your
blood alcohol level is above the legal limit. Also, your
reactions are likely to be the wrong ones in an
emergency.

It isn't that difficult to remember to drive on the
left-hand side of the road; after all, everyone will be
doing it. The times you are most likely to forget are
when turning a corner or when emerging from a car
park (parking lot), and in complicated urban driving.

Driving on the left

If you are driving a British car, you may actually
have more trouble driving on the 'wrong' side of the
car. First, you have to remember which side of the car
to get into. Then the various controls are likely to be
on the opposite sides of the wheel from what you're
used to: you may find yourself turning on the
windscreen (windshield) wipers instead of the turn
signal. The foot pedals *are* in the same order,
however, You may also catch yourself looking into
the wrong mirror when backing up or having

difficulty estimating the distance from the kerb (curb).

If you have brought over a car designed to be driven on the right-hand side of the road, you may have a little trouble seeing when trying to pass a car or when entering a roundabout (see below), or in judging distances when turning right. It helps to have someone else in the car with you to tell you when the way is clear.

Speed limits

Speed limits are not posted on main intercity roads. All you will see is a round white sign with a black diagonal slash through it, which means that the national speed limit applies. This means 70 mph (113 kmh) on motorways and dual carriageways (divided highways), and 60 mph (97 kmh) on other main roads. Cars towing caravans (trailers) are limited to 50 mph (80 kmh) on these roads. The speed limit in built-up areas with street lights is 30 mph (48 kmh); this is usually posted only as you enter cities and towns. Other speed limits will be posted on round signs. A particularly quaint one says 'DEAD SLOW' (which you should interpret as meaning about 5 mph). Speeding is a national vice – very few people obey the signs, which is odd for such a law-abiding nation.

Round-abouts

A roundabout is a traffic circle in the middle of an intersection. Its purpose is to keep traffic flowing without resorting to stop signs or traffic lights. However, it works effectively only when there is an even flow of traffic from all directions; in some places the traffic planners have had to admit defeat and install traffic lights too. Some roundabouts are huge 'gyratory' systems, having smaller roundabouts within them; others are just circles painted on the road (mini-roundabouts), which some people drive over in defiance. Many normal-sized roundabouts are very nicely landscaped.

Roundabouts may look confusing at first, but they operate on a very basic principle: you drive in a clockwise direction, yielding to traffic coming from the right that is already in the roundabout. Before entering the roundabout, signal left or right as you would at a normal intersection (if you are going off in either of those directions). Once on the roundabout, signal left before you go off so that people waiting to get on will know if you are continuing on around or not.

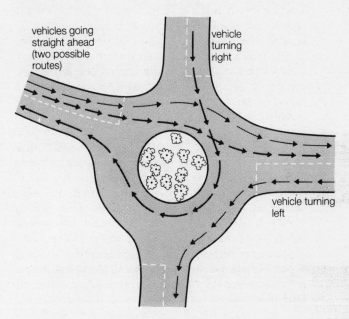

vehicles going straight ahead (two possible routes)

vehicle turning right

vehicle turning left

A roundabout, showing how to turn right and left and go straight ahead

Roundabouts with only one lane of traffic are simple to manage. If there are more lanes, however, you must get into the correct one for the direction you'll be going off. Lanes are sometimes marked with arrows on the road surface to help you with this. If you want to take the first road to the left, stay in the left lane. To go straight ahead, use either of the left two lanes (the outside lane is recommended on two-lane roundabouts). If you are taking the road off to the right, use the right lane and continue around in that lane, changing to a left lane (making sure there's no one coming up behind you) before exiting.

On very large roundabouts, the lanes may be marked with road numbers or place names so that you don't have to think too hard. One good thing about roundabouts is that if you miss your exit, you can go around again – making sure you are in the appropriate lane, of course.

Some roundabouts may have more than four roads coming off them or there may be more lanes going around than going off. In some places there are two small roundabouts in a row: treat them separately and yield to traffic already in the second one when you get to it. Try to move quickly onto and around roundabouts if you don't want to annoy other drivers.

Traffic lights

English traffic lights are similar to those in most other countries, though they are always on posts, never hung on wires above the road. One difference is that the red and amber (yellow) lights are both on at the same time just before the light turns green, which gives you advance warning of the change. When only the yellow light is on, the signal will next turn red.

Some intersections with traffic lights have a 'filter' sign for left turns, meaning that you can turn left on a red light when safe. Otherwise, turning left on a red light is *not* permitted.

Intersections

When two cars coming from opposite directions are both turning right at a junction (intersection), they are supposed to pass *behind* each other unless the layout of the junction makes that difficult. Watch to see what other cars are doing.

Yellow crisscrossed lines in an intersection mean that you must keep that area clear. That is, don't enter the area unless you're sure you can get out of it by the time the traffic signal changes, and don't stop on the lines in a queue of traffic.

There are two types of pedestrian crossing: the zebra crossing (a striped crosswalk) and the pelican crossing (with pedestrian-controlled lights) (see p. 65). Cars must stop for people who are on these crossings and should wait until the people have gotten across completely. Drivers may continue through a pelican crossing if the light is flashing yellow and no one is still on the crossing. You are not allowed to overtake another car just before a crossing, nor can you stop on a pedestrian crossing. You must also give way to people who are crossing the road when you are turning a corner.

Road markings

A solid white line across the road at an intersection is a stop line, while a broken white line means that you must give way (yield) to traffic on the other road. An inverted triangle on the road also indicates that you must give way ahead.

The normal lane marking is a single broken white line, meaning you can pass when it's safe to. Long lines with short gaps indicate a hazard ahead (like a bend in the road, an intersection, etc.), and you should not pass another car then unless you're very sure the way is clear. On a two-lane road, a solid white line on your side of the middle means that you are not allowed to pass.

Bus lanes are labeled as such on the road surface and are separated from other lanes by a very thick white line. Note that bus lanes operate both with and against the flow of traffic. You are allowed to drive in bus lanes outside of the posted bus hours.

Signs

Most traffic signs are clear in meaning and rely on pictures rather than words (most are used internationally). In general, circular signs with a red border indicate some restriction and triangular signs give a warning of some kind. *Give way* means 'yield,' and *way out* means 'exit.' (See p. 76.)

Parking

It is often not easy to park on the street in inner London during the day, and parking in other cities isn't much better. There are car parks (parking lots), of course, but these may not be close to where you want to be. Some car parks use a 'pay and display' system, whereby you have to guess how many hours you'll be parked and hope you have the correct change to put into the machine. You then receive a sticker to put on the inside of your windshield.

'No parking' areas are marked in a variety of ways.

National speed
limit applies

Outlined in red:

Maximum speed | Give way to traffic on major road | No right turn | No left turn | No U turns | No overtaking | No stopping (clearway)

No entry for vehicular traffic | No motor vehicles | No motor vehicles except solo motorcycles, scooters, or mopeds | No cycling | No pedestrians | Give priority to vehicles from opposite direction

Cross roads | Roundabout | Staggered junction | Traffic merges from left | Slippery road | Change to opposite carriageway (may be reversed) | Right-hand lane closed (symbols may be varied)

Two-way traffic straight ahead | Road narrows on right (left if symbol reversed) | Dual carriageway ends | Road works | Loose chippings | Pedestrian crossing

DANGER | Train crossing without barrier or gate ahead | Location of train crossing without barrier or gate

On blue background:

Ahead only | Turn left ahead (right if symbol reversed) | Turn left (right if symbol reversed) | Keep left (right if symbol reversed)

One-way traffic

Mini-roundabout (roundabout circulation — give way to vehicles from the immediate right) | Vehicles may pass either side to reach same destination | Route to be used by pedal cyclists only

Some common road signs

The *clearway* sign, a blue circle with a red *X* through it, means that you can't park or stop along that section of the road. Yellow lines along the side of the road indicate a parking restriction. Double yellow lines mean no parking at all, except during posted hours, if any. A single yellow line means no parking during working hours (usually 8 a.m. to 6 p.m. Monday through Saturday). Broken yellow lines mean no parking during posted times; look for the signs explaining the restriction. You also must not park on the white zigzag lines leading to a pedestrian crossing.

At night you should park facing the direction of the traffic. Avoid parking directly opposite another parked car on a narrow road. If you have to park with your wheels on the sidewalk on a narrow road, make sure there is ample room for pedestrians. Also make sure that you haven't parked on a street that is reserved for residential permit holders only (this will be signposted).

If you park illegally in some areas of London, you may not only get a ticket, but also find a nasty wheel clamp attached to your car, which prevents you from moving the car. You must then report to the police station indicated and pay a large fine before your car will be set free.

City driving

Owing to the lack of residential garages and parking lots near local shops, cars are often parked along one or both sides of the streets, narrowing them to one lane. If the obstacle is on your side of the street, you should give way to oncoming cars. If there are obstacles on both sides, the car nearest to a place to pull over normally does so and signals to the other car to proceed by flashing its headlights.

If you are thinking about driving in London, think again. Traffic is heavy; street layouts are confusing; London drivers tend to be impolite; and the main north and south circular routes are very congested, especially where three lanes go into two with no warning. Public transportation is far more relaxing. In many other cities, the one-way systems in the central areas make it difficult to get to where you want to go.

Roads
Motorways

Motorways are limited-access, multilane roads. They are marked in blue on almost all maps and the motorway number is preceded by the letter *M*. They cannot be used by student drivers, cyclists, moped riders, people on horses, or hitchhikers. The far right lane should be used only for overtaking. Trucks and cars pulling trailers are not allowed to use the right-hand lane on a three-lane motorway. You cannot overtake a car from a slower lane, that is, from the left – you must always overtake on the right-hand side of the vehicle you're passing. If it is blocking your way, move behind the car and wait for it to move into a slower lane; you can flash your lights at it, but do not blow your car horn.

The hard shoulders are to be used only for emergencies, not for picnics or taking photographs. There are emergency phones placed at one-mile intervals all along the motorways, and posted arrows indicate the direction of the closest one, so if you break down, you rarely have far to walk to get help.

Motorway lanes are marked with *cats' eyes*, which reflect oncoming headlights in the dark. White cats' eyes indicate the lane markings; yellow ones run along the right-hand edge of the highway; red ones on the left-hand edge separate the lane from the shoulder; and green cats' eyes mark the entrance to a slip road (ramp).

Older and some newer motorways are notorious for constantly being under repair. The M1 (the main north-south motorway) never seems to be free of roadworks; even the newly built M25 around London is undergoing repairs. In roadwork areas, a 'ramp' sign indicates a bump in the road. Road surfaces in general are not as good as many Northern European roads, but they are better than many in the U.S.

Service areas can be found along most motorways, although not along the M11 and M25 yet. These areas provide fuel, fairly good food (self-service restaurants and snack bars), clean toilets (including toilets for the disabled and areas for changing diapers), and a small shop or two. Signs on the motorways tell you how far it is to the next one.

'A' roads are primary routes that range from divided
highways to slower two-lane roads. They are usually
marked in red on maps. Along such roads you can
find chain restaurants such as Happy Eater or Little
Chef, which provide fast, reasonable food in clean but
standardized surroundings; petrol (gas) stations; frequent *lay-bys* (places to pull off the road, but often
without facilities or even wastebins); but not many
toilets, and few of them clean. Small trailers used as
tea and food stalls are sometimes parked in lay-bys,
serving a small selection of hot and cold snacks. On
country roads you may also find roadside stalls
selling farm produce such as free range eggs, honey,
soft fruit and flowers. Parking places are signposted
with a *P*. *'A' roads*

It is fairly common along 'A' roads to see
hitchhikers who are holding up car license plates.
Such people are employed to drive new cars with
temporary plates to car dealers and are paid to take
the train home. They hitch in order to save the train
fare.

'B' roads are secondary country routes with only one
lane of traffic in each direction. They are marked in
yellow on most maps. 'Other' roads (in white on
maps) are narrow and sometimes only single-lane. On
smaller roads in the depths of the countryside you can
encounter such interesting obstacles as shallow
unbridged fords, unguarded railway crossings, and
animals being herded along the road. You must watch
out for people riding horses and bicycles. *'B' roads and
lesser roads*

Single-track roads with frequent passing places are
common in very rural areas. When two cars meet,
whichever is the nearest to a passing place must pull
into it, even if that means backing up (but don't make
a bus or truck back up). It is important, obviously,
never to park in a passing place.

Many minor roads are resurfaced with gravel, so if
you come across new surfacing, drive slowly and stay
far behind the next vehicle.

Routing signs give distances only in miles, in spite of
Britain being in the EC. A route number or place *Route signs*

name given in parentheses on a sign means that the road you are on will lead to a turnoff for that destination. Blue routing signs are used for motorways, green for primary routes, and white for others.

Gas stations   Petrol (car fuel) is graded by a star rating indicating the amount of octane it contains. The ratings are:

2 stars (∗∗) = 90 percent octane

3 stars (∗∗̇) = 94 to 96 percent octane

4 stars (∗∗̈) = 97 to 99 percent octane

Most European countries use a two-grade octane system, so if you have brought a car from the Continent, you will need to know which octane level the car needs. As yet, there are very few stations that carry unleaded fuel. Diesel fuel is widely available, and goes by the name of 'derv.'

Petrol stations are fairly abundant except in rural areas. It can, however, be difficult to locate one that is open on a Sunday. Most are modern, self-service affairs. Depending on the station, the petrol pumps either each have a specified octane level or else allow you to choose the right octane level by pressing a button. Full operating instructions are displayed on the pumps. Some stations still sell petrol by the imperial gallon, but many have gone over to liters (see p. 205). To pay, you have to go into the station, where you can often also buy candy, soft drinks, snack food, toys, maps, etc. Don't always expect to find toilets, however. Where they are provided they tend to be basic, cold, and not always clean or well-provided with paper.

There will usually be a bucket of water and a brush and paper towels available for cleaning your windshield, but automatic car washes are not that common. Stations should and normally do provide an air line for filling up tires.

Garages   If you need repair work done on your car or even just a tyre (tire) mended, you must go to a garage (some of which also sell petrol). Many specialize in certain makes of car. If you only know the American terms for car parts, the following may be helpful in communicating with English mechanics:

U.S.	British	U.S.	British
hood	bonnet	a flat	a puncture
trunk	boot	wheel rim	wheel
bumper	fender	side-view mirror	wing mirror
muffler	silencer	windshield	windscreen

There are companies that will replace broken windscreens immediately for you wherever you are on the road. The two main automobile clubs – the Automobile Association (AA) and the Royal Automobile Club (RAC) – provide breakdown services for drivers who hold membership in an auto club in another country. Otherwise, you have to phone a garage if you have trouble on the road.

Accidents

Accidents must be reported to the police if someone is injured. Call 999 from any telephone for police and ambulance. If you have any kind of accident involving someone else, get their name and address and their vehicle's registration number before leaving the scene. If anyone else saw the incident, try and get their names and addresses too, just in case any legal action is taken. Notify your insurance company as soon as possible.

Understanding the natives (and being understood)

Many first-time visitors to England who arrive secure in the knowledge that they know the English language discover after a few minutes that they can't understand very much of what the natives are saying. The problem is that neither many years of learning English as a foreign language nor a lifetime of speaking American or Australian English can prepare you for the surprising number of ways in which English is actually spoken by the people in the country where it originated. Tourists who claim that they 'just love the British accent' don't realize just how many different accents there really are!

For such a small country, England has, over the centuries, developed a very wide range of both regional and social accents and dialects. The natives seem to cope quite well with this diversity. However, most foreigners have been exposed to only one form of British English. This variety, often referred to as 'Oxford English' or 'the Queen's English,' is the form usually taught to Europeans and most often heard on radio and TV. It is actually very much of a minority accent, spoken mainly by the aspiring middle classes and by the upper classes. If you plan to speak to ordinary English people – porters, taxi and bus drivers, shopkeepers, publicans (bartenders), and the like – you will have to cope with other accents. But don't be dismayed – you'll soon get the hang of them. The trouble is that as soon as you move somewhere else, sometimes even as little as 15 miles away, you may have to get used to a new one. Take consolation in the fact that in most areas of the country, the really difficult varieties are confined to older and more rural inhabitants, who you probably won't come into contact with.

Visitors who don't know any English will be at a

real disadvantage, because there is very little provision for people who don't understand and speak at least some English, though many educated English people do know a smattering of French, and perhaps some German. Generally, if you speak in a foreign language, you will be answered in loud, slow, but not unfriendly English.

Accents

Almost any English person can pinpoint the area of the country that other natives come from as soon as they open their mouths. Differences between accents can be vast; no native would ever mistake, say, a Londoner for a Yorkshireman.

Some features common to most British accents cause difficulties for foreigners. In most accents, r is not pronounced unless it comes before a vowel, so *part* sounds like 'paht' and *car* like 'cah.' Even more confusing is the habit of inserting an r between vowels where it does not belong: English people say 'the idear of it,' 'Americar and Canada,' and 'drawring.' Words like *tune* and *duke* can also cause difficulty, because in most places they end up sounding like 'chune' and 'juke.' *Schedule* is often pronounced with an initial 'sh.' However, North Americans are always impressed by the 'careful' way that many English people pronounce their t's, as in 'Brittish' (not the North American English version, 'Briddish').

The following is an attempt to give you some idea of the kinds of differences you can expect to find between accents (though, of course, generalization can't cover all eventualities).

The Queen's English

The Queen's English (posh English) is the variety spoken by most national TV and radio announcers, by those educated at Public Schools (private schools; see pp. 189–90), by the upper and upper-middle classes, and of course by the Royal Family. Linguists label this variety RP, which stands for 'received pronunciation'; that is, 'received' in the best circles.

Despite exposure to this type of accent, many North Americans have trouble understanding it. One of the biggest difficulties involves the vowel sound in words like *top*, *off*, and *wrong*. Such words are pronounced with rounded lips, so the vowel sounds like something between 'oh' and 'aw.' Another problem is the *a* in words like *half*, *dance*, and *tomato*, which is pronounced as that in *father*.

There is also an affectation – or a widespread speech impediment – found in certain upper-crust circles which involves pronouncing *r* rather like *w* (thus, 'bwing me my bwandy, Bwian').

Cockney   Tourists who visit London will probably be confronted with the intriguing sounds of the Cockney accent. It can also be heard on TV, in films, and in the theater, spoken by lower-class east Londoners. Cockney is often looked down upon because of its social connotations.

The accent can be quite difficult to understand at first. Pronunciations that seem to throw the uninitiated involve both vowels and consonants. The dropping of the *h* at the beginning of words gives forms like 'im' for *him* and 'ear' for *here*. *Th* gets pronounced like *f* or *v*, as in 'bofe' for *both*, 'fing' for *thing*, and 'fevva' for *feather*. Sometimes *l* sounds almost like *w*, as in 'miwk' for *milk* and 'feow' for *feel*. At the end and in the middle of words, *t* often comes out as a glottal stop (like the sound at the beginning of *'uh-'uh*), so that *bitter* sounds like 'bi'ah' and *cat* like 'ca'.' Many vowels and vowel combinations are pronounced differently, too: *play* can sound more like *ply*, *a boat* like *about*, and *by* like *boy*.

West Country   A distinct series of accents can be found in areas to the south and west of London. Speakers of these varieties actually do pronounce the *r* in words like *part* and *car*. In Bristol, the largest city in the west of England, an *l* gets added to words ending in *a*: older Bristolians visit 'Canadal' and 'Americal'; they eat 'pizzal' and 'vanillal' ice cream, and drink tea out of 'chinal' cups; and then there were the three Bristol sisters called Evil, Idle, and Normal!

The eastern part of England, to the north of London *Eastern* and including the cities of Cambridge and Norwich, is notable for pronunciations such as 'who' for *Hugh* and 'voo' for *view*. It is in this part of the country where you may hear 'boo'iful moosic.' In Norfolk, words like *boat*, *soap*, and *go* sound suspiciously like *boot*, *soup*, and *goo*.

The accents of the Midlands and the North of *Northern* England are distinguished from those of the South by two main characteristics. One is the vowel in words such as *up*, *butter*, and *flood*, which is pronounced like that in *put*, *could*, and *took*. That is, *buck* is pronounced the same as *book*, and the pairs *put* and *but*, *good* and *blood*, *pull* and *hull* are rhymes. The other characteristic is that, in these areas, words such as *dance* and *path* have the same vowel sound as in *cat*. (Northerners tend to look down on the posh, effete-sounding southerners who say 'dahnce' and 'pahth.')

In the Birmingham, Manchester, and Liverpool areas, the *g* is actually pronounced in words like *singer* and *thing*. And in the accent of Liverpool (called Scouse), *t* often sounds like *ts*.

Yorkshire accents are notable for pronunciations such as 'mek' and 'tek' for *make* and *take*, and for the omission or reduction of *the*, as in the stock phrase 'There's trooble at'mill.' In the Northeast, around Newcastle, where the natives are for some strange reason known as Geordies, the accent can be especially confusing for foreigners (and even for southern English people). The vowels are the main problem, with pronunciations like 'oowa' for a long *o* (giving 'boowat' for *boat*) and 'eeya' for a long *a* (as in 'feeyat' for *fate*).

Welsh English has a distinctive intonation pattern, *Welsh English* which the English describe as being 'lilting' or 'singsong' in nature. Consonants in the middle of words seem to be drawn out in pronunciation, as in 'cit-ty' or 'mon-ney.' The Welsh English *r* sounds different from the English *r*, and is more of a flap. The vowels are pretty much the same as in southern

English varieties, except that the *a* in *dance*, *path*, etc., is like that in *cat*. The Welsh are fond of ending sentences with the tag *isn't it* (as in 'You're going to the show tonight, isn't it?').

Scottish English

The vast majority of Scottish people pronounce the *r* in words like *part* and *car* but, as in Welsh English, this is a flapped *r*. Almost all Scottish vowels are a bit different from English ones. For example, *caught* is pronounced like *cot*, *Pam* like *palm*, and *pull* like *pool*. However, *fern*, *bird*, and *hurt* represent three different vowel sounds. Scots use a distinctive consonant in Scottish words like *loch* (lake) and *Sasanach* (Englishman): the *ch* is pronounced like a breathy *h*. In addition, they pronounce *wh* at the beginning of a word as 'hw.'

Devotees of Robert Burns's poetry will be familiar with Lowland Scots dialect pronunciations such as 'hoose' for *house*, 'doon' for *down*, 'hame' for *home*, 'dee' for *die*, and 'day' for *do*. Lowland Scots differs from other varieties of English in a large number of other features of pronunciation, grammar, and vocabulary, making it almost impenetrable to outsiders.

Stress

The placement of stress in British English sometimes differs from that in North American English and is often the source of misunderstandings and general amusement. Words of French origin usually have very un-French stress in British English, with the emphasis falling on the beginning of the word: *BALlet*, *BATon*, *GARage*, *DEBris*, *St. BERNard*. Words ending in *-ary* and *-ory* often have later stress and/or have an abbreviated ending in English accents: *laBORatry*, *anCILLary*, *SECretry*, *STRAWbry*. Compound words tend to have the emphasis on the second word: *weekEND*, *iceCREAM*, *hotDOG*.

Vocabulary

People who know North American English will find that English people use unfamiliar words for some familiar items. There are, in fact, so many of them that special dictionaries have been published to cope with the problem. To give you some idea of the range of differences, here are just a few examples (others are mentioned throughout the book):

British	North American
Alasatian (dog)	German shepherd (dog)
biro	ballpoint pen
candyfloss	cotton candy
cling film	Saran Wrap
cutlery	silverware
draughts	checkers
drawing pin	thumbtack
fortnight	two weeks
full stop	period
ground floor	first floor
hairslide	barrette
inverted commas	quotation marks
jumble sale	garage/rummage sale
kitchen roll	paper towels
Lilo	air mattress
nappy	diaper
nought	zero, nothing
plimsolls	sneakers
row (rhymes with *now*)	argument
rucksack	backpack
sellotape	Scotch tape
torch	flashlight

More confusing, perhaps, are the many British English words that look the same as North American English words but either mean something completely different or have a different primary meaning (secondary meanings are given after semicolons below):

	British meaning	North American meaning
basin	bowl	sink
a billion	a million million	a thousand million
biscuit	cookie or cracker	baking-powder roll
braces	suspenders	dental devices for straightening teeth
caravan	trailer	convoy
cheap	inexpensive	substandard; inexpensive
dumb	mute	stupid; mute
egg rolls	bread bun with egg in it	Chinese spring roll
fancy dress	costume	formal attire
homely	homey	plain or ugly

jelly	Jell-O	clear fruit jam
jumper	pullover, sweater	dress worn over blouse
just about	only just	not quite
knickers	women's underpants	knickerbockers
knock-up	awaken by knocking on door	make pregnant
mad	crazy; angry	angry; crazy
mind	be careful of (as in 'mind your head')	do what someone tells you
muffler	thick neck scarf	silencer for car exhaust system
nervy	nervous	bold
pancake	crêpe	thicker fried-batter mixture
pants	underpants	trousers
pavement	sidewalk	roadway
pudding	general dessert	custardlike dessert
quite	moderately; very	very
rubber	eraser	condom
sherbert	fruity powdered candy	fruity ice dessert (British *sorbet*)
smart	well groomed	clever; well groomed
surgery	doctor's/lawyer's/politician's office; an operation	an operation
tights	panty hose	dancer's or skater's legware
vest	undershirt	waistcoat

Some Britons are also fond of using archaic forms like *amongst* and *whilst*.

In most parts of the country, older and more rural people still use dialect words and sentence structures that may be obscure to people elsewhere. Most natives are aware of these, however, and tend not to use them around foreigners.

Rhyming slang   Londoners, especially those on the fringe of the law, use a peculiar sort of sublanguage known as *rhyming slang*. This has found its way into general usage in the rest of the country and even as far away as Australia, and can be heard on TV shows depicting criminals or working-class Londoners. The way it works is that one word is represented by a phrase of two or more words that somehow go together and in which the last word of the phrase rhymes with the intended word. Thus, *butcher's hook* stands for *look* in rhyming slang. Very frequently the phrase is reduced to its first element, so that *butcher's* comes to represent *look*, as in *'Ave a butcher's at this, guv*. A few of the better-known rhyming slang terms are:

rhyming slang	*'normal' word*
loaf (loaf of bread)	head
dicky bird	word
trouble and strife	wife
whistle (whistle and flute)	suit
apples (apples and pears)	stairs
Brahmsed (Brahms and Liszt)	pissed (drunk)
tod (Tod Sloan)	alone (as in 'to be on your tod')

Spelling

Most spelling differences between British and North American English are either well known, like *colour* vs. *color* and *theatre* vs. *theater*, or else cause no difficulties in understanding, such as *travelling* vs. *traveling*, *realise* vs. *realize*, *licence* vs. *license*, *enquire* vs. *inquire*, *tyre* vs. *tire*. There are a few, however, that can cause some confusion. For example, criminals are sent to *gaol*, not *jail*; farmers use *ploughs*, not *plows*; and houses with poorly sealed windows get *draughts*, not *drafts*.

Using language

After staying a while in England, you may find that you are able to tell roughly which part of the country someone comes from. You can also readily identify someone's social background and status simply from the way that person speaks. The biggest giveaway is accent – the more regional a person sounds, the lower his or her social status is likely to be.

There are also some words and phrases that are stereotypically associated with social class. There is some truth in the idea that the upper classes have a penchant for overstatement, for example, and tend to describe things (very loudly) as being *terribly interesting*, *awfully nice*, *frightfully boring*, *smashing*, and *jolly wonderful*. Such people are still careful to use *one* instead of *you* for general reference (one must be firm about not letting one's standards slip, mustn't one?), and to avoid 'common' terms like *toilet* and *serviette*, preferring the posher versions *lavatory* and *table napkin*.

The English strike many foreigners as being extremely polite (at least until they try to get served in a shop), an impression caused mostly by the enormous frequency with which the British say *please* and *thank you*. In fact, they say *thank you* so often that some abbreviate it to *ta*. They say *please* when handing their fare to the bus driver, although he or she rarely says *thank you* back. At shops, customers say *please* when handing their purchase to the clerk, to which the clerk says *thank you*, followed by the customer saying *thank you* when receiving the goods, and the clerk saying *thank you* again. The English say *sorry* even if you stand on their feet or bump into them. They say *excuse me* if they want you to move out of their way.

You will have to be prepared, according to your age and sex, to have strangers call you things like *dear*, *love*, *duck*, *flower*, and *hen* (up north) if they feel well disposed toward you. Londoners call men of higher social standing *guv* (for *governor*).

If they are not well disposed toward you, then you may be called a variety of other terms, including *wally*, which isn't obscene, or *pillock*, *prat*, or *wanker*, which are, or be told to *piss off* (go away). The English insult people nonverbally with a two-finger gesture that resembles the V-for-Victory sign with the palm turned inward, given with a slight upward motion of the arm. (This is very rude, and is on par with the American one-finger gesture or the southern European one-arm gesture.) So if you want to indicate *two* of something, make sure you don't perform this gesture by mistake. Words to avoid that are rude in England include *fanny* (many Americans get into trouble using this – it refers to the female genitalia, not the backside) and *bloody*, which is a quite strong swearword.

The English are less keen on euphemisms than many other peoples and can seem quite insensitive or blunt in their use of words. The inheritance tax is called the *death duty*; people over sixty-five are *old-age pensioners*; people who are hard of hearing wear *deaf-aids*; and certain types of handicapped people are called *spastics*. There are institutions called the Hospice for the Terminally Ill and the Hospital for Sick Children (why else would they be there?). On the other hand, the English don't like to talk about the workings of their intestines, and quite often complain about stomachaches that have nothing to do with their stomachs.

When telling time, the English custom is to say, for example, 'ten *to* six' and 'ten *past* six.' English people are confused by Americans who say 'ten *of* six'; they can't figure out whether this means ten minutes before or after the hour. On the other hand, the English sometimes say 'half six' for 6:30 and succeed in confusing those Europeans for whom half six means 5:30.

Times and dates

Dates are normally written with the day first, then the month and year: 7th November, 1986. The order is the same when the date is just in numerals: 7/11/86 (which is different from the North American practice). A phrase like *Tuesday week* means 'a week from Tuesday,' and *a fortnight Monday* means 'two weeks from Monday.'

Almost all tourists fall flat on their faces when trying to pronounce English place names. It is bad enough that London is called 'Lundn' and the river Thames is the 'Temz,' but there's also:

Place names

'Dahby' for Derby
'Lester' for Leicester
'Sawlsbry' for Salisbury
'Wooster' for Worcester (whose 'oo' is pronounced like that in *book*, not *fool*)

In general, -*shire* in county names is pronounced as 'sheer' or '-shuh'; -*cester* is reduced to '-ster'; -*ham* is '-um'; -*burgh* and -*borough* are '-bruh' or '-burruh'; -*wich* is '-idge', and -*wick* is often '-ick.' Some pronunciations, however, are completely unpredictable. Quite often in place names of three or more syllables, one syllable is dropped altogether (as in Happisburgh becoming 'Haysbruh'). The word *Saint* in place names (and personal names) is unstressed and sounds something like 'Snt.' Probably the best thing to do when asking for a potentially unpronounceable place is to just point to it on a map or write it down.

Village names can be interesting, perplexing, and highly amusing. Sometimes villages grouped close together share one element of a name and are distinguished from each other by some descriptive (and often olden) term:

Burnham Overy, Burnham Deepdale,
   Burnham Norton, and Burnham Thorpe
Much and Little Hadham
Over, Middle, and Nether Wallop
Sidford, Sidmouth, and Sidbury (all on the river Sid)
Toller Fratrum, Toller Porcorum, and Toller Whelm

Thus a sign that says 'The Willbrahams' is intended to lead you to a group of villages sharing that name, not to someone's house.

Other names, such as Cley-next-the-Sea, Owmby-by-Spital, and Widecombe-in-the-Moor, are geographically quite precise but are a real mouthful. And some are just plain funny. How would you like to live in Blubberhouses, Foul Mill, Great Snoring, Mop End, Piddle, or Ugley?!

It may be helpful to know that someone who comes from Liverpool is a Liverpudlian, and a person from Manchester is a Mancunian.

Eating out

The Hungarian humorist George Mikes, long resi- **English** dent in England, once wrote that 'on the Continent **cuisine** people have good food; in England people have good table manners.' Indeed, very many foreigners labor under the impression that it is not possible to find good English food in restaurants and thus end up going to those serving French or Italian or other international food.

Stereotypical English cuisine includes overdone meat drowned in thick gravy, vegetables that have been boiled to death, stodgy (heavy) desserts, and greasy fried fish with soggy fried potatoes. All of this is, of course, untrue. The quality of English cooking is variable, but it *has* improved in recent years, both in the range of foods available and in the preparation of them.

Good traditional English cooking tends to be simple, relying on fresh seasonal produce with hints of herbs and seasonings. Main courses are often served with a dab of a piquant condiment or sauce (mustard, horseradish, red currant jelly, etc.) rather than being smothered in a fancy rich sauce.

There has been a resurgent interest in traditional regional dishes. Some that are more widely found include Lancashire hot-pot (a sort of lamb stew); beef cooked in cider; homemade Cornish pasties (pastry filled with minced meat, onion, and potatoes); black pudding (sausage made from oatmeal, herbs, and blood, which tastes better than it sounds); herrings in ale; and various savory pies. Each region seems to have its own special and tempting varieties of steamed puddings, fruit pies, and cakes.

Secure in the knowledge that it *is* possible to find **Where to** good English food, you must then take the time to *find it* locate a place serving it at a reasonable price. Frankly, not many restaurants do. Expensive restaurants serve Continental cuisine for the most part. Books such as *The Good Food Guide* are very helpful for locating more up-market places serving English cuisine, while *Just a Bite* (Egon Ronay) and *The Good Pub Guide* include less expensive venues. Some of the best food can be found at simple country inns, especially at lunchtime on Sundays. Probably it is best to avoid restaurant chains – the food will be okay but on the unimaginative side and with few fresh vegetables. Restaurants post a copy of the menu outside so that you can see what is offered at what price. They may also post signs on the window that boast 'A taste of England' (or Devon or Yorkshire, etc.), which indicate that traditional recipes are used; or they may state that their food is homemade.

Eating hours   English eating hours may seem very restrictive to many tourists. Breakfast is usually served from 8 to 9:30 a.m.; lunch is from 12 a.m. to 2 or 2:30 p.m. (office workers usually take their break from 1 to 2 p.m., so avoid that hour if possible); afternoon tea goes from about 3:30 to 4:30 p.m.; and dinner runs from about 6:30 to 10 p.m., with 8:00 being a fashionable time to start. If you are hungry at 5:30 p.m. or want to have a very late meal after a show, that's just too bad – you'll probably have to settle for fish and chips or Chinese take-away (carry-out/take-out). And even the fast-food shops normally aren't open all day long, although they do stay open late at night to catch the crowds after the pubs shut. There are few twenty-four hour cafes, and most cater to truck drivers (that is, they serve fried food and chips with everything). There are some 'family restaurant' chains along main travelers' routes (in particular, Little Chef and Happy Eater), which are open from 7 or 7:30 a.m. to 10 p.m.

On Sundays, many restaurants (including fish-and-chip shops) are closed all day, while others may be open only for traditional Sunday lunch. You can usually find Indian or Chinese restaurants open on Sundays, and some pubs may offer hot food in the evenings.

The adage about children being seen and not heard has a stricter interpretation in English restaurants – they don't think children should even be seen! You aren't allowed to take children under fourteen into a pub for a meal unless there is a separate family room, which may be a shock to may Europeans. Children are, of course, allowed in restaurants, but it isn't customary to take them out to eat, except perhaps for Sunday lunch or on a special occasion. Few eating establishments make any effort to accommodate children with special menus, smaller portions, high chairs, or the like – children are more tolerated than welcomed. The only places where you may be made to feel genuinely welcome if you have children with you (with the exception of hotels, which expect them) are fast-food restaurants and places run by people from more family-oriented cultures (Chinese, Greek, Indian). The English attitude is changing, but it has a long way to go in this respect before it catches up with other parts of the world.

Eating with children

You would be well advised to book (reserve) a table at a restaurant on a Friday or Saturday night or for Sunday lunch. If you are in a large city, however, you'll probably find somewhere to eat without a reservation if you just wander around.

Reservations

Once in a restaurant, you should usually wait to be seated. (At your hotel's restaurant you may be assigned a table for all your meals and can just seat yourself upon entering.) At some restaurants and pubs with restaurants, you may be asked to wait in the lounge area and have a drink while looking at the menu, and won't be taken to your table until your meal is ready. In an inexpensive restaurant you may occasionally be asked to share a large table if the place gets too crowded, and it is considered impolite to refuse to do so.

Unfortunately, restaurants rarely have a no-smoking section.

Common sense should tell you the standard of dress to adopt for a particular restaurant – you don't wear scruffy jeans into the Savoy, but you can wear them

Dress

to a roadside cafe. Older Britons tend to dress up when going out to eat, especially on a Sunday: men wear ties and women wear nice dresses. Some snooty and expensive restaurants demand that men wear a tie but may lend you one if you come without it. Mostly, just about anything goes, as long as you are fully clothed and shod (wearing shoes).

Table settings

Tables are set with an impressive array of silverware. Start with the outer pieces and work your way in, always using two utensils (except when eating soup). Different types of knives and forks are used for fish and for meat dishes, so you may be brought a new set of cutlery after you place your order. However, you will rarely be given a steak knife (and that isn't because the meat is so tender that you don't need one). The cutlery for dessert, a spoon and a fork, is placed above the plate. Coffee spoons are brought with the coffee.

Tables are usually set with salt (in the shaker with only one hole), white pepper (fresh black pepper in a grinder is not found in many restaurants), and English mustard (which is very hot) to accompany meat. There may also be a bottle of malt vinegar on the table in restaurants that serve chips (fried potatoes).

Service

Don't expect waiters and waitresses to be chatty or very friendly. They might be, but that kind of behavior isn't *expected*. They are usually efficient rather than fawning.

Eating style

Americans always comment on the strange way that the English eat. Actually, it is the Americans who have a peculiar way of eating – the rest of the Western world eats like the English. The fork is held in the left hand, with the tines curving downward, and the knife is held in the right. Neither is set down between bites. The knife is used both to cut food and to guide it to the fork. The fork is not used for cutting or scooping up food in polite circles (although it can be so used, held in the right hand, to eat food which doesn't need cutting). Don't feel that you have to try eating this way, but if you don't you'll probably find that everyone else will have finished eating before you have.

Drinks

Most restaurants are licensed to serve alcohol. Those that aren't often allow you to bring your own wine, but this isn't done at licensed premises.

The most common before-dinner drinks seem to be sherry, gin and tonic, lager (beer), and wine. Fancy cocktails are not normally requested, but may be available.

You aren't usually brought a glass of water at the table unless you specifically ask for it, and it most likely won't come with ice. In fact, few drinks are graced with ice, even in the summer, unless you ask.

Many people have wine or lager with their meal, if they have anything to drink. Most wines are from the Continent, although California wines are creeping onto the menus. You won't find English wines served in restaurants – there *are* some wines made in England, a few of which have won international prizes, but they just aren't offered in restaurants. Prices of wines in most eating establishments are enormously inflated.

Of course, you don't have to have something alcoholic to drink. Milk, mineral water, juice or

"The wine should be chilled, Benson. Stand it by the door for a few minutes."

Reproduced by permission of *Punch*

squash (artificially fruit-flavored drinks), and perhaps some other soft drinks may also be available. Milk shakes, if you can find them, are made just with milk and flavoring, not with ice cream. Iced tea is unheard of, and coffee is not usually drunk with the meal but is taken after dessert.

Menus   In the more traditional restaurants, menus are divided into *à la carte* (from which you chose individual items for each course – more expensive) and *table d'hôte* (a narrower choice of set meals, for a set price).

Appetizers   The range of starters varies from place to place, of course, but you will almost always find 'prawn cocktail' on the menu. This consists of shrimps (or small prawns) drowned in a mayonnaise-based sauce. Fruit and fruit juice, pâte, soup, and smoked fish are also common.

Bread rolls may be brought around to the table, but they usually aren't warm. Salads are not that common, nor very interesting (although they are improving, and salad bars are on the increase). The choice of salad dressings is not extensive, with French dressing (oil and vinegar with herbs) being the most common. Salad cream, similar to runny mayonnaise, is also popular.

Main course meats   One of the most typical of English dishes is roast beef and Yorkshire pudding (a very light batter mixture baked in the oven), served with horseradish and gravy. Your roast generally comes medium to well done. Roast lamb is also popular, and is accompanied by a mint and vinegar sauce. Roast pork comes with applesauce. Gammon, a thick cut off the thigh of the pig, like ham, is often served with pineapple rings. For those who like a variety of meats, there often is a mixed grill, consisting of sausage, bacon, liver, kidney, and a lamb chop – a cholesterol lover's dream.

If you are used to American or Australian beef, English steaks may be disappointing, since they can be tough, tasteless, and expensive (though Scottish beef is considered to be good). Prices should tell you

the relative quality of steaks: a fillet steak (pronounced 'FILLit'), which is the same as a fillet
mignon, is the highest quality, with sirloin and rump
steaks also being good quality. Meat is cut differently
in England than in various other countries, so the
names of cuts may not be familiar, or familiar names
may refer to slightly different cuts. (You won't find
T-bone, porterhouse, rib eye, and Delmonico steaks,
or other 'exotic' cuts.) It *is* possible to get good,
tender, tasty steaks in England, but it seems to be a
matter of coincidence rather than consistency in any
one area.

More down-to-earth but interesting meat dishes,
such as meat pies, are popular and usually flavorful
and quite affordable. Steak and kidney (or steak and
mushroom for the squeamish), chicken and
mushroom, and ham and turkey pies are all standard.
Game pies, made from pheasant, rabbit, or venison,
can be found in season (autumn and winter) and are
highly recommended. Shepherd's pie is a hearty dish
made of minced (ground) lamb or beef, with onion
and maybe carrot, and topped with mashed potato.

Poultry

Poultry, like red meat, is usually roasted. For some
strange reason, the English don't think of poultry as
meat and insist on serving small sausages and/or
bacon with it, as well as covering it with dark gravy.
Accompaniments for poultry include bread or sausage stuffing and bread sauce (a thick white creamy
mixture with cloves in it). Roast duck is of variable
quality in restaurants; roast pheasant can be found in
season, often with very tasty and interesting accompaniments.

Fish

Fresh fish ought to be available in a good number of
areas, but many restaurants still serve frozen fish.
Grilled Dover sole and lemon sole are specialties (it's
sacrilegious to have them fried), and whole trout grilled or pan-fried with almonds is also popular. If you can
afford fresh salmon, it's of excellent quality. Salmon
often comes poached or wrapped in pastry. Most
other types of fish are served fried, but you may be
able to persuade the chef to grill it for you if you prefer.

Fish pie is a good, homey dish, usually consisting of white fish chunks, onion, and mushrooms in a white sauce, topped with mashed potatoes. Fresh eel pie and jellied eel can also be found in a few places.

Shellfish (usually prawns and crab) generally appear on menus as starters rather than as main dishes. Scampi is the exception, but it is almost always deep-fried. If you do find main-course shellfish dishes, you may have to get over the shock of their price, and they may not be made with fresh shellfish, either.

Vegetarian food

Vegetarians may have difficulty finding an interesting variety of offerings at many English restaurants. Omelettes, quiches, and salads with cheese or egg may often be your only choices, with the occasional bland pizza thrown in. You will, however, be able to find good vegetable dishes at the many Indian and Chinese restaurants. London and some university towns have a smattering of real vegetarian restaurants, which are increasing in popularity.

Vegetables

Main-course salads are popular for light dinners and in the heat of the summer (if there is one). These consist of some type of cold meat, smoked fish, or cheese along with a green salad and perhaps other kinds of salads or pickled vegetables. Americans should note that, for instance, chicken salad means chicken *with* salad, not the U.S. version in which the chicken is cut up and combined with mayonnaise.

If you like potatoes, you will be happy with typical English fare. With many meals, particularly roasts, you get two or more kinds of potato: roast, baked (but not with sour cream), sautéd, mashed, or chips (thick, soft french fries). The natives sprinkle chips with malt vinegar, but it is possible to get ketchup or mayonnaise to put on them if you ask.

Many cheaper restaurants serve frozen vegetables instead of fresh. In general, fresh vegetables tend to be plain boiled ones, but they are sometimes served with garlic butter or cheese sauce. It is common for a selection of vegetables to be served in more traditional restaurants.

Dessert portions can be quite substantial, so remem- *Desserts*
ber to leave room for some. In posher restaurants a
sweets trolley stacked with a wide choice of goodies is
wheeled before you to break down your willpower.

   Dessert offerings usually include such delicious
things as gateaux (layer cakes with cream filling), fruit
tarts or flans (a pastry or cake base with fruit and a
thin layer of glaze on top), fruit salad, one flavor of
ice cream or sorbet, and some sort of trifle. This last
popular dish is made with various types of desserts in
layers: sponge cake soaked in sherry under custard or
Jell-O with added fruit, topped with whipped cream
and nuts. Other traditional English desserts are
syllabub (lemon, cream, sugar, and sherry or wine
whipped together), fruit fool (stewed fruit blended
with cream), and heavy, cakelike steamed puddings
such as plum pudding, jam roly-poly, bread and
butter pudding, and spotted dick (with currants in it).
Steamed puddings are served with hot, runny, yellow
vanilla-based custard poured over them. Waiters
often have to be restrained from pouring cream over
your dessert, even over cake and fruit salad. Ice cream
and whipped cream toppings are not as common.

Cheese and biscuits (crackers) are served instead of or *Cheese*
after dessert. In some places you are allowed to help
yourself to whatever cheese you want, while in others
you will be served a portion. The cheeses are usually
French or English. Native cheeses such as Cheddar,
Gloucester, and Red Leicester are firm and mild;
Stilton is a stronger blue cheese. Apples and other
fruit are sometimes served with the cheese.

After the sweets course at upmarket restaurants you *Savories*
can also opt for some kind of savory dish, usually
something on toast, such as kidneys, sardines, scram-
bled egg, or Welsh rarebit (cheese sauce).

After all that food, you may order coffee or tea. The *Coffee*
coffee is quite strong by American standards but
weak by European. Most English people put milk in

their coffee – this is known as 'white' coffee. Waiters
will ask if you want your coffee 'black or white'
rather than 'with or without milk'. Brown sugar is
served with coffee, and white sugar with tea.

Most licensed restaurants will offer a selection of
liqueurs after coffee.

Paying   When you want to pay, ask for the *bill*, not the check.
VAT (Value Added Tax), currently 15 percent, will
automatically be added to the total. You can include a
10 percent tip if no service charge has already been
added and if the service warrants it. Tips are not
expected at breakfast or for quick snack meals. Most
restaurants now accept at least some of the major
credit cards.

International   In addition to the many restaurants serving Con-
cuisine   tinental food – and, in London, serving Greek,
Hungarian, Japanese, Middle Eastern, and just about
any other kind of food you can think of – England
abounds in Chinese and Indian restaurants. Many of
these have a take-away (take-out) service as well as
normal restaurant service.

Chinese food is a good value for the money. Most
is Cantonese, since the majority of Chinese people in
England come from Hong Kong. Other regional
varieties can be found, though, especially in London.
If you want to eat with chopsticks and from rice
bowls, you often have to ask for them. English
Chinese restaurants do not serve fortune cookies after
the meal.

Indian restaurants are also good, inexpensive places
to eat. Don't be put off trying them if you don't
know anything about Indian food: the menus usually
describe each dish, specify the degree of spiciness, and
include mild dishes. They also often offer 'English'
food such as steak and chips, burger and chips, or egg
and chips for the unadventurous.

Restaurants with American-sounding names and
decor usually bear no resemblance to their American
counterparts. They may serve cocktails, hamburgers,
and steaks, but the food tastes very little like
American food.

Along with Chinese take-away, the indigenous national fast food is fish and chips, and it is not to be missed. Fish-and-chip shops vary in quality, but the fish is usually good if the shop is attached to a wet fish shop (one selling fresh fish).

Fast food
Fish and chips

The fish is coated in batter and deep-fried in very hot oil so that it is crisp on the outside but succulent inside. Fish and chips is served wrapped in white paper. You are supposed to unwrap it, put salt and a generous amount of malt vinegar on it, and eat it with your fingers. Sometimes effete little wooden or plastic forks are available for those who prefer using a utensil.

A board in the shop will tell you what kinds of fish are available: the most common are cod, plaice, haddock, and skate. To order one piece of, say, cod, and a portion of chips, you simply ask for 'cod and chips.' To get two portions wrapped separately, ask for 'cod and chips twice'. You can also just order chips on their own by asking for a specified number of pence worth (there will usually be prices on the board).

Fish cakes, meat pies, sausage rolls, spring rolls (Chinese egg rolls), chicken pieces, pickled onions, and hot mushy peas can also be bought at many fish-and-chip shops.

The American hamburger chains McDonald's, Burger King, and Wendy's have been springing up around English cities, providing successful competition to the English chain Wimpy. The English are still getting used to fast-food restaurants and haven't yet figured out that they are expected to clear their tables when finished. The Anglicized American chains often make you pay for a packet of ketchup, and you usually must ask for other condiments.

Hamburgers

Other U.S. fast-food restaurant chains that have invaded the country include Kentucky Fried Chicken (which is vastly inferior to the American version) and Pizza Hut. While London has some good pizza parlors, many serve quite bland pizzas, so Pizza Hut seems good by comparison.

Other

For a quick snack, a pub or bakery can be just the place to go. These often sell sandwiches, filled crusty rolls, sausage rolls, and sometimes hot and cold individual meat pies. Beware, however, that if you are very hungry, English sandwiches are less generously filled than American ones.

Many department stores have cafeterias where you can get snacks or even full-cooked meals. Near beaches and tourist sites, you can often find tea stalls that sell sandwiches, burgers, and so on, and ice cream vans (see also 'pub food,' p. 114–15).

Cafes   There are two sorts of cafes: transport cafes, or 'caffs,' which cater to truckers and other working people and serve things like egg and chips, sausage and chips, meat pie and chips, steak and chips, etc. and chips, with baked beans or peas thrown in for good measure; and *cafés*, or tea shops, with lace curtains, tablecloths, and cut flowers, which serve morning coffee and afternoon tea to middle-class ladies and tourists, among others.

You will not find many Parisian or Mediterranean-type cafés with outdoor tables and tolerant waiters who let you sit and sip one coffee for hours while reading a book. English weather, the narrow sidewalks, and the crowded interiors militate against this.

Wine bars   Wine bars are the current trend in cities and towns. Besides offering wine they often have nice light snacks, such as salads, quiche, or soup, and hearty sandwiches, and are usually good value for your money. They tend to be inhabited by trendy young business people.

Tea   Everyone knows that England is a nation of tea drinkers. A majority of the inhabitants probably start the day with a 'cuppa' and take a tea break sometime around 4 p.m. Tea is also offered in times of crisis, when there is no whiskey at hand. Hot tea can be surprisingly refreshing, even on a warm day.

Most English people put milk (*not* cream) into their tea (although not into exotic or herbal teas); but don't feel that you have to follow this custom. However, milk will automatically be put into your cup unless you ask for your tea 'black.' You also must specify if you want your tea weak, because it tends to come fairly strong. You will be offered a choice of teas only in smarter places.

When you order a pot of tea, you'll usually be brought two pots: one with the tea brewing in it (often just a tea bag, with no strings for easy removal) and the other with hot water to replenish the teapot. If the teapot does have loose tea in it, a strainer will also be provided. A small jug of cold milk is also included. There is huge controversy in England over whether you should pour the milk into the cup before or after the tea, but in the end it makes no difference. Should you want a slice of lemon for your tea, you are more likely nowadays to be able to get one, although some English people may still regard this as heresy.

Afternoon tea, especially in a tea shop, is not just a cup of tea – there are also various goodies to be consumed. One standard item is the *scone* (pronounced either 'skone' or 'skon'), a soft, raised flour-and-egg mixture that sometimes contains currants or sultanas (white raisins). (It resembles an American baking-powder biscuit.) Scones are often served warm and are eaten with butter and jam. Fruitcake, sponge cake, buns (sweet rolls), and crumpets (flattish yeast bread with holes, served toasted – like American so-called English muffins) are also served with tea. In fancy tea shops, thin delicate sandwiches made out of cucumber soaked in vinegar, or egg and garden cress, are the thing to have.

'Cream tea' is *not* tea with cream in it. It is a repast which includes a highly calorific and delightful kind of thick, spreadable cream that you put on your scone along with the butter and jam and have with your tea. Although this cream goes by the unappetizing name of 'clotted cream,' few people can resist its temptation. Cream teas are popular in rural and tourist areas, and are a particular speciality of the southwest.

Some hotels and restaurants serve *high tea*. This is not to be confused with afternoon tea at 4 p.m. High tea

High tea

is served around 5 to 5:30 p.m. and is really a light dinner. The main course may be a salad with cold meat, a light grilled dish, or poached fish. After that, the tea goodies roll out. High tea is the grand version of the meal known simply as *tea*, which many working-class people eat in the early evening if they have a large dinner at lunchtime (which they call dinnertime). If you find this confusing, that's because it is. If someone asks you around for tea, try to figure out from the time you are supposed to be there which kind of tea it is – a cup of tea or a light dinner.

Pubs

The pub (public house) is the focal point of social life for many English people. It is not just a place to drink, but a place where they can easily bump into friends, make new acquaintances, find out what's been going on in the area, and put the world right. Pubs are a good place to go if you are having difficulty meeting the natives, for there is something about the atmosphere of a pub that makes the typical English reserve melt away (although it may be up to you to open the conversation).

Neighborhood pubs abound, reflecting the social makeup of the area, while pubs in town and city centers may each attract a different sort of patron (you can usually tell as soon as you walk in whether or not it is your sort of crowd). Drinkers tend to have a favorite 'local' that they go to; established 'regulars' may even keep their own special beer mug at the pub.

Pubs vary enormously, from rough, smoky watering holes to cheerful and welcoming country inns to trendy bars selling exotic cocktails. Most are very open in design, with no secluded corners or booths; at crowded times (lunch and after 10 p.m.) you can easily find yourself sharing a table or padded bench with strangers. Many pubs display interesting items on the walls, on railings, or suspended from the ceiling – horse brasses, bottles, and old tools are among the more popular items. Lighting tends to be subdued, making it a shock to the system when you go out into the cold light of day after a relaxing lunchtime drink. Toilets are usually small and cold.

There are normally two halves to a pub: the public bar, and the lounge or saloon. The bar side is seen as being suited to working-class males; the beer is a penny or two cheaper, the furnishings more basic, and the smoke thicker. Games (see 'entertainment,' pp. 115–16) are often located on this side of the pub. The lounge is better furnished and more elaborately decorated than the bar. This is the side that 'ladies' are supposed to stay on. Some pubs will also have a few tables and chairs outside for warm-weather use.

Particularly in the north of England, women have traditionally not been encouraged to go into pubs on their own. This attitude is changing, however. It is perfectly safe for women to go into pubs alone, but they may get 'chatted up' (flirted with).

Hours   Pubs keep very restrictive business hours. These were set by law during World War I to keep the population more sober and healthier, but today they seem to frustrate natives and visitors alike and force people to drink too much too quickly. Most English pubs are open from 11 a.m. to 2:30 p.m., and then from 6 p.m. to 11 p.m., Monday through Saturday. On Sundays, they are open from 12 noon to 2:30 p.m. and from 7 p.m. to 10:30 p.m. Local opening times may vary by a half hour or so, but all pubs are supposed to close by 11 p.m. This ensures that the publican (landlord), who often lives above the pub, can clean up and recover before the next day's work.

On Christmas Eve, Boxing Day, New Year's Eve, and other special occasions, pubs can extend their closing hour to 12:30 or 1 a.m. to allow their customers time to celebrate to the fullest.

You'll know when closing time is near because the landlord will ring a bell, toot a horn, or make some other loud noise and announce: 'Last orders, please.' That is your cue to rush to the bar to buy your final drink. At closing time, the bell (etc.) will sound again and the landlord will yell, 'Time, gentlemen, please' (sometimes ladies get a mention as well). This will be followed shortly by 'Drink up now, please.' Legally, you have ten minutes after closing time to finish whatever your are drinking, but some landlords start stacking tables, turning out lights, unplugging the jukebox, and opening doors to encourage customers to leave. Others wait patiently until the last drinkers crawl out.

The afternoon closing times mean that you cannot

get a beer at a pub in England in the middle of a hot summer's day. You can buy it in many grocery stores or at an off-license (liquor store), but on Sundays only during licensing hours. If you aren't near a shop, or if you just want to sit down and be served, your only alternatives are to go to a cricket match or take a short train trip – licensing hours don't affect either of these.

If you haven't had your fill of drink by the time the pubs close at night you can pay to join an 'after hours' club in many larger towns and cities. Some of these are disco-type places, while others are simply late-night pubs. Restaurants will serve alcohol outside of licensing hours with food, and hotels and inns can serve their residents alcohol any hours they choose.

Drinking age

You must be eighteen to be served alcohol in England. However, you are allowed to go into a pub at the age of fourteen if accompanied by an adult. You won't be asked to show anything to prove your age – the English don't carry any form of identification – but if you are suspected of being underage, you won't be served.

Some pubs provide a children's room (with no bar in it) so that parents can come to the pub without having to get a baby-sitter. Families can always sit at tables outside the pub, and indeed are forced to if there is no family room; but the weather isn't always hospitable enough for this nor are there always enough outside seats. Although children under fourteen are excluded by law from the part of the pub serving alcohol, they can go inside to use the toilet. Some publicans will allow parents with babies in the pub. The restrictions against children in pubs probably have less to do with worry about the corruption of five-year-olds or the possibility that they might be served drinks than with the fact that many men go to pubs to escape their families.

Beer

The majority of pubs are tied to (owned by) particular breweries and serve only that brewery's beer. Freehouses are owned by individuals and sell a range of beer brands. There are hundreds of breweries

"Do me a favour! How do you expect me to keep ice in this heat!"

Reproduced by permission of *Punch*

in England; about a half dozen are big nationwide companies, while the others are smaller regional or very local breweries.

If you are eager to try authentic English beer, go to a pub advertising *real ale*. Real ale is 'live' beer; that is, it has live yeast in it. It is conditioned in the cask and must be kept properly in the pub cellar at about 55°F (not 'warm,' but uncomfortably close to English room temperatures!), or else it will 'go off.' The beer is 'pulled up' by a hand pump, which is harder to do than it looks – barmen and barmaids have well-developed biceps. Real ales are not fizzy at all, and most have a very full flavor. They are not only unique in taste, but some also have exceptional names: Old Peculier, Mad Monk, and Bishop's Tipple are just a few of the more unusual.

Real ales had almost died out in England by the

1960s, and were being replaced largely by pasteurized, carbonated keg beers. Carbonated beers are more consistent in taste and easier to keep than the live real ales, but most beer lovers didn't like the taste (or lack of it) or the fizziness. Lately, real ales have made a comeback. A book called the *Good Beer Guide* will steer you to pubs selling the real stuff.

Pubs usually offer around four different types of beer on tap (more in a freehouse). Beer is also sold in bottles. By far the most popular type of beer is *bitter*, a pale, somewhat bitter drink that contains about 4 percent alcohol. There are different 'grades' of bitter – often both an 'ordinary' and a 'best' or 'special' will be available. The nearest bottled equivalent to draft bitter is *light ale* or *pale ale*, although the bottled varieties are a bit fizzy.

Mild, which is harder to find, is darker, weaker, smoother, and a bit sweeter than bitter. Its bottled equivalent is *brown ale*. *Strong ale* is just that – strong flavored and higher in alcohol content (about 5.5 percent). *Stout* is also higher in alcohol content and is very dark, heavy, smooth, and sweetish. The best-known brand of stout is Guinness. *Barley wine* is like sweetish concentrated beer, and comes in small bottles.

Lager, which is gaining in popularity, is available everywhere, but may be weaker than the European counterparts. It is served colder than ordinary English beer, but not really ice-cold.

Beer mixtures are quite popular. Here are some of the more common ones, which may go by slightly different names in different areas of the country: *Mixtures*

brown and bitter:	bottled brown ale mixed with draft bitter
half and half:	bitter and mild
black and tan:	Guinness (or other stout) and bitter
black velvet:	Guinness and champagne (or stout and cider for the less wealthy)
shandy:	bitter and lemonade (a fizzy lemon soda) or ginger beer – especially popular in hot weather
lager and lime:	lager and lime cordial
lager and black currant:	lager and black-currant-based mixer

Ordering   Ordering beer in a pub can be somewhat daunting – it is in such situations that you can really feel foreign. After elbowing your way to the bar (there is usually no waiter service), you have to get noticed. The best way to do this, especially for women, is to hold your money in view and look desperate.

You cannot, of course, just ask for 'a beer.' You'll have to choose the type, as described above, and in freehouses also the brand. You can always ask one of the patrons for advice on what is best, which is also a good way to start up a conversation.

Beer is served in half-pint and pint glasses – you cannot (usually) buy a pitcher or jug of beer to take to a table and share. Some people are particular about the type of glass they drink out of – one with straight sides or a mug with a handle – and the bartender may ask you which you prefer. Traditionally, women are expected to drink half pints (if they drink beer at all), and will often be given it in a glass with a stem. Men seem to be in awe of women who drink pints of beer out of straight glasses.

When ordering, ask for 'a half' or 'a pint' of whatever type of beer you want. If, for example, you want two pints and a half pint of the same kind of beer, you ask for 'two pints and a half'; if you want one pint and two halves, say 'a pint and two halves.' Ask for each type of beer separately, instead of reeling off a huge list of drinks at once. When ordering draft Guinness as well as other beers, ask for the Guinness first, because it takes much longer to fill the glass and the bartender has to keep scraping the thick foam off the top.

Your last difficulty (after paying) will be returning to your spot without spilling the beer. This is made difficult both by the crowds and by the fact that there is no foam on English beer (except Guinness), so the glasses are filled to the top or to a line near the top of the glass. You can ask for a tray (and should bring it straight back to the bar), or just deliver the drinks in stages.

It is normal to take your empty glass back to the bar for a refill if you're having the same thing again.

Each person in a group usually buys a round of drinks, so if you are with three Britons, you can expect to have three drinks bought for you. This means you must pace your drinking accordingly, perhaps sticking to a half pint initially. Don't forget to say 'cheers' to the person who has bought the drink. You don't tip the barman or barmaid, but you can, if you want, offer to buy him or her a drink.

Other drinks

Of course, you don't have to drink beer at a pub. Most also serve a range of spirits (gin, whisky, vodka, etc.), liqueurs, cheap wines, and nonalcoholic mixers.

Whisky means Scotch whisky in most places. (If you prefer Irish whiskey, Canadian whisky, rye, or bourbon, you have to specify and hope that they have it.) Most pubs stock more than one kind of Scotch, so ask for it by name. There are around 100 different brands of malt whisky and dozens of blended whiskies manufactured in Britain, many of which can only be found in Scotland. If you drink your whisky undiluted, ask for it 'neat.' You can also have it with ice (but don't say 'on the rocks' – you might not be understood) or mixed with dry ginger ale, both of which are considered desecrations of good Scotch. It is more permissible to have it with a little water.

Cocktails are only just catching on outside of London. Gin and tonic has always been popular and rum and coke is certainly known, however. Bloody Marys are also common, but may consist just of vodka and tomato juice, although you may be asked if you want Worcestershire (pronounced 'woostershire') sauce and a slice of lemon. If you ask for a martini, you'll be given a glass of Martini brand vermouth. Other more exotic cocktails probably won't be known by name except in posh hotels or those places that specifically call themselves cocktail bars. (For instance, a screwdriver is just known as vodka and orange juice.) If you want a cocktail that isn't too complicated to make (that is, doesn't have exotic ingredients or require a blender), the bartender will probably be happy to make it for you if you know the right proportion of elements.

Cider   Most pubs also offer draft or bottled cider. Don't be fooled into thinking that cider is just apple juice: it is very alcoholic, and can go to your head quickly on a hot day. *Scrumpy* is a particularly potent type of cider from the West Country. Cider comes in both (slightly) sweet and dry varieties, and is either sparkling (fizzy) or still (flat).

Food   Almost all pubs sell snacks such as peanuts, potato crisps (potato chips) in various flavors (e.g., salted, salt and vinegar, cheese and onion, bacon, scampi),

"Have you any crisp-flavoured crisps?"

Reproduced by permission of *Private Eye*

and pork scratchings (fried pig skins). Some also sell candy bars. A few pubs are lucky enough to be visited by roving shellfish vendors, who wander through offering small portions of cold shrimp, mussels, cockles, etc.

Having a meal at a pub can be an inexpensive way to satisfy your hunger. Pubs that do serve food will advertise the fact. Menus are usually available at the counter. You order at the bar, paying when you order.

Cold pub meals tend to consist of filled bread rolls or sandwiches, cold meat pies, ploughman's lunch (cheese, bread, a little salad, and pickles), and cold meat salads. Other cold offerings may include Scotch eggs (hard-boiled egg rolled in sausage meat and bread crumbs, then deep-fried) and pickled eggs.

Hot meals range from just 'basket meals' to full dinners. The former is usually fried scampi or fried fish or sausage with chips. Cornish pasties, sausage rolls, and jacket (baked) potatoes are also common. Some pubs specialize in homemade dishes such as hearty soups, meat pies, curries and chili. Others branch out to full main courses with two or three vegetables. Some pubs set up 'carving rooms' at lunchtime, serving a variety of roast meats with vegetables and salads, and on Sundays, many country pubs serve traditional full roast dinners at 1:00.

Pubs that serve food usually also serve coffee. And besides food and drink, most pubs also sell cigarettes and cigars.

Entertainment

Many pubs have a games room and may even sponsor organized teams that compete against other pub teams. A pool or billiards table is a standard fixture in larger pubs, while a dart board can be found in almost every pub (see p. 165 for rules). Cue sticks and darts are often available at the pub, but keen players bring their own. To get a game, you may have to put your name on a board and play the winner of the previous game.

Skittles, a miniature version of 10-pin bowling, is popular in some country pubs, especially in the southwest. You can also find regulars playing cribbage and dominoes while they drink.

Much to the annoyance of many customers, pubs now usually have fruit machines (slot machines) and electronic games, which make loud noises.

Music comes most often from a jukebox, although some pubs have live music one or two nights a week. Others may provide a piano for the more uninhibited drinkers to display their talents or lead the assembled drinkers in a sing-along.

Names   Every pub hangs a sign outside announcing its name (with an appropriate picture) and the name of its brewery. In some cases it's hard to tell which is the pub name and which is the brewery's: for example, Greene King is a brewer while the Green Man is a pub. There seem to be few generalizations you can make about pub names, although they aren't named after their landlord.

Many pubs take their names from royalty, animals, or local features: e.g., The Queen's Head, The Old Dun Cow, The Bridge. Others refer to local trades or tools of the trades: The Baker's Arms (as in coat of arms), The Beetle (mallet) and Wedge. Some enumerate items or even name abstractions: The Three Tuns (beer barrels), The Moderation. Then there are amusing combinations for which it is hard to imagine any explanation: The Eagle and Baby, The Frog and Nightgown, The Hog in Armour, The Queen's Head and Artichoke, The Slug and Lettuce, Ye Trip to Olde Jerusalem. Just ask in the pub, and no doubt someone will tell you the story behind the name.

Shopping

Shops range from extensive department stores to tiny boutiques, from huge supermarkets to small market stalls. In most city and town centers, major stores are concentrated along a few main roads and are referred to as the 'high street' shops. Colorful open-air markets still survive in some localities, and more often than not are set up in a central location. They vary in size and frequency of opening, but tend to be once a week and to offer a wide range of goods at reasonable prices: fresh fruit and vegetables, meat and flowers, clothing, records, books, antiques, household goods, and junk.

Rows of small shops can be found in most residential areas; they usually include a butcher, baker, greengrocer (fresh fruit and vegetables), general grocer, newsagent, chemist (pharmacy), sub-post office, and sometimes a fishmonger (fresh fish), ironmonger (hardware), laundromat, off-license (alcohol), bank branch, turf accountant (betting shop), pub, and fish-and-chip shop or Chinese take-away. On the outskirts of larger cities and towns, superstores are springing up, which combine the offerings of large supermarkets and small department stores, thus sparing suburban residents from using the crowded city centers. Rural dwellers, however, can rarely avoid trips into their larger neighboring towns, for the small village shops supply a limited range of goods, supplemented in some areas by fresh fruit and vegetable vans that sell to regular customers.

City and town shopping is usually not a very relaxing experience. Since the shopping areas tend to be centralized, greater concentrations of people use them than in the U.S. and Canada. The narrow pavements (sidewalks) get crowded quickly, and

there is no unwritten rule that everyone should keep
to the right or left on the pavement or stairways.
Stores rarely have automatic doors to aid those
burdened with small children or shopping bags.
Inside the shops, aisles tend to be narrow. And the
shop assistants (clerks) are notorious for being
uninformed, unavailable, and unhelpful – the English
do not like to serve.

Hours Most shops are open from 9 a.m. to 5:30 p.m.
Monday through Saturday. The early closing time
means, of course, that shops are packed on Saturdays
because that is the only time working people can get
out. Some towns are experimenting with late-night
shopping (usually till 8 p.m.) one night a week, often
on a Thursday, and many superstores are open past 6
p.m. Some small grocery shops (often run by
non-Anglo-Saxons) stay open in the evenings most
nights and on Sundays. Off-license stores (selling
alcohol) are open in the evenings, usually until 9 or
9:30 p.m.

Local shops may close for lunch between 1 p.m.
and 2 or 2:30 p.m. Stores that are outside of large
town centers may also observe 'early closing day,'
usually on a Wednesday or Saturday, when they are
open only in the morning. This affects sub-post
offices as well as stores.

Sunday is supposed to be a day of rest, supported
in law by the Shops Act of 1950, which prevents most
things from being sold on a Sunday. There are many
anomalies stemming from this legislation: you can
buy a newspaper or a soft-porn magazine on Sunday
but not a Bible; you can buy alcohol but not milk;
razor blades but not razors; fresh vegetables but not
tinned (canned) ones; Chinese take-away food but
not fish and chips; and so on. Some discount
furnishing, gardening, and DIY (do-it-yourself)
stores do open on Sundays at the risk of being fined.
Sunday markets are allowed to operate in some areas,
and grocery stores run by non-Christians can do
business as long as they close one other day of the
week. Hardly anyone is happy with this state of
affairs, but an attempt to change the law in 1986

failed, and it now seems possible that the Sunday trading laws will begin to be more vigorously enforced.

General shopping

Popular English souvenir items include bone china, wool sweaters, tweeds, linen tea towels, antiques, tea, marmalade, biscuits, and raincoats. There are items to suit almost every taste and budget; but remember that street 'bargains' may not turn out to be so wonderful when you get them home.

The price of all goods (except children's clothes, raw food, and books) includes VAT (Value Added Tax), now at 15 percent. If you buy expensive items to take out of the country with you, you can avoid paying this tax by asking the store clerk for a VAT 'personal export' form when you purchase the goods. However, not all stores carry these forms, and some will give them to you only for purchases over a

Reproduced by permission of *Punch*

certain amount. You must show your passport to get the form. When you leave the country, you show the goods and the form to the customs officials and then send the stamped form back to the store. Larger stores often will ship nonportable purchases home for you and take care of the VAT exemption paperwork. Note that VAT exemption applies only to goods purchased within three months before you leave.

In London, many tourists head for one of the big fancy stores, often just to look since prices can be high. Harrods (in Knightsbridge) is probably the best known. They say you can buy anything from 'a pin to an elephant' there; certainly the offerings are vast and varied. The food hall is especially worth visiting, not just for the marvelous selection of food but also for the decor. Fortnum & Mason (Piccadilly), another well-known store, specializes in exotic foods and employs assistants who wear green tailcoats. Selfridge's (Oxford Street) and Liberty's (Regent Street) are the other big attractions, the latter especially for exclusive printed fabrics. Children will be delighted to visit Hamley's (Regent Street), a vast toy store. HMV (Oxford Street) is Europe's largest record store, carrying all sorts of LPs, while Gramophone Exchange (Wardour Street) has one of the largest stocks of classical records in London. Cartier (Bond Street) is *the* place to go for jewelry. There are numerous very good spots for shopping in London, from exclusive boutiques to arcades, like the old Covent Garden market, to street markets. Many guidebooks (Fodor's, for example) give detailed accounts of specific stores and shopping areas.

Various national and regional chain stores throughout the country sell good merchandise. Marks and Spencer sells reliable if fairly conservative clothing for adults and children, as well as high-quality fresh foods. British Home Stores, C & A, Littlewoods, Debenhams, and Woolworth's are found in many sizable towns and stock clothing and (except for C & A) household goods. Stores in the John Lewis Partnership (they go under various names) are department stores that sell quality goods of all kinds, from clothing to household items, gifts, appliances, yarns, and much more at reasonable prices.

While department stores have an interesting and wide **Department** range of goods, popular items often seem to be out of **stores** stock. Clerks will check to see if the item you want is in stock if you ask, but they never seem to know when the next shipment is coming in. If you do order something (especially a large item), you may have to wait two or three weeks or even a month for delivery, even for goods made in England.

Department stores tend to be crowded. They are often equipped with escalators going up but not necessarily going down – you have to use the stairs or the lifts (elevators). Remember that the floor at street level is the 'ground floor,' the one above that is the 'first floor,' and so on. Most large department stores have public toilets but not drinking fountains. Some have cafeterias.

Department stores generally do not supply gift boxes or offer gift-wrapping services. However, they often do give you the clothes hanger when you buy clothing.

English clothing is sturdy and well made; indeed, **Clothing** Saville Row suits are world-famous for their excellence (and for their expense). Off-the-rack clothing may be cut a bit differently from what you're used to, so try it on before buying. For instance, the hips in women's clothing are cut a bit narrower than in North American clothes. It is not easy to find women's petite sizes or fashionable attire for 'oversized' people. Only upmarket stores offer alteration services.

Clothing labels often give measurements in inches (sometimes also in centimeters), as well as assigning an overall size. You can try on items, of course, but do not be surprised if you have to use a communal dressing room in shops catering to younger tastes. Marks and Spencer does not allow customers to try on clothes, but you can return anything that doesn't fit.

The following chart gives equivalents for various national sizing conventions, but note that this is really only a rough guide to middle-range sizes.

women's dresses, blouses, sweaters, skirts
(British 14 = bust 36 in/91 cm hips 38 in/97 cm)

British	10	12	14	16
American	8	10	12	14
French/German	36	38	40	42
Spanish/Portuguese	38	40	42	44
Italian	40	42	44	46

women's shoes

British	4	5	6	7
American	$5\frac{1}{2}$	$6\frac{1}{2}$	$7\frac{1}{2}$	$8\frac{1}{2}$
European	36/37	37/38	38/39	39/40

men's sweaters, suits, coats
(British size = chest measurement in inches)

British & American	36	38	40	42
European	46	48	59	52

(men's trouser sizes go by the waist measurement
and the inside leg (inseam) length, in inches)

men's shirts (British size = neck size in inches)

British & American	15	$15\frac{1}{2}$	16	$16\frac{1}{2}$
European	38	39	40	41

men's shoes

British	8	9	10	11
American	$9\frac{1}{2}$	$10\frac{1}{2}$	$11\frac{1}{2}$	$12\frac{1}{2}$
European	41/42	42/43	43/44	44/45

Drugs and toiletries   Boots chemist shops (pharmacies) appear every-where, selling toiletries, baby supplies, health and restricted-diet foods, candy, household goods, records, books, and other items, as well as dispensing medicine. Other chemist shops and drugstores tend to just fill prescriptions and sell nonprescription medicines and toiletries. Drugstores do not even have a registered pharmacist on hand. Some medical supplies may be called something other than what you are used to: for instance, acetaminophen is *paracetemol*; rubbing alcohol is *surgical spirit*; Band-

Aids are *sticking plasters*; and vitamin is pronounced 'VITTamin.'

Many towns have excellent small bookshops that are well stocked and run by knowledgeable salespeople. London is particularly good for second-hand bookshops. In general, books written in foreign languages are not so easy to locate.

Books and records

One of the largest chains selling popular books is W H Smith, found in most towns of any size. (These stores also sell newspapers, magazines, stationery supplies, and records.) For academic and hard-to-find books, the best places are Dillons in London, Blackwells in Oxford, and Heffers in Cambridge. In their volume and coverage, these stores are hard to beat. You can also buy books in department stores, but the selection is generally limited.

General, specialized, and second-hand record shops are easy to locate in most sizable towns; some are part of a larger store. The albums and tapes themselves are not on display, just the record jackets and empty cassette boxes, to prevent damage and shoplifting. When you've made your selection, you take the empty container to the counter and get it filled.

Most record and book stores operate a gift-token (gift-certificate) system. The way it works is that you buy a paper record or book token for a specified amount of money and stick it in a special card. The person receiving the token can then redeem it at almost any book or record store anywhere in the country. Other stores have copied this system, and you can now buy tokens for general purchases at particular shops.

You can find shops that sell newspapers and magazines both in the main shopping districts and in rows of local shops. Those in cities or town centers usually have a larger selection, and in London they may also have foreign newspapers. People also sell local and Sunday newspapers from designated spots along the sidewalks in the the town centers.

Newspapers and magazines

A newsagent's shop is rarely just a newspaper and

magazine outlet. It may also be a stationer's, a tobacconists's, a confectioner's, or a combination of these. Stationers supply such items as greeting cards, postcards, wrapping paper (sold by the sheet from a rack), biros (pens), batteries, a few books (mostly romantic fiction), and of course stationery. Tobacconists sell cigarettes, cigars, etc., as you would expect, but note that you must pay for matches. A confectioner sells candy by the box or bag or even by weight from large jars like in old-fashioned sweet shops. Many newsagents also have a small freezer in which they keep ice cream bars and the like, and may also sell soft drinks.

If you want to have a newspaper or magazine delivered to your door, make arrangements with the nearest newsagent's shop. You can pay for the papers at the shop on a regular basis. Sunday papers have to be ordered separately from week-day papers (see pp. 174–75).

Electrical goods

Most electrical appliances sold in England have no plug. This is because there are two types of socket: the older style, which takes two round pins, and the modern one, which takes three-blade plugs. Also, many of the items are sold throughout Europe, where plug styles change from country to country.

When you buy a three-blade plug you will also need to know what size fuse to put in it for that appliance – usually 3, 5, or 13 amp. If it doesn't state the size on the appliance, ask the clerk.

If you plan to take an electrical item home with you, make sure that the wattage and voltage are compatible with your system there. English electrical lines carry 220 to 240 volts, while North American and Japanese carry only 110.

Putting on a plug

It's a little daunting to put on a plug for the first time. What if you do it wrong? (You'll get a shock, or it just won't work.) All you need is a small screwdriver and a small amount of intelligence. Most electrical goods come with wiring instructions anyway, and some plugs have wiring codes inside them.

The electrical cord on the appliance should have

two or three different colored strands coming out, each with about one-quarter inch of bare copper wires at the end (if not, cut back some of the colored plastic to reveal the wires). Unscrew the back of the plug by loosening the single screw in the middle. Loosen the other two screws that hold the retention collar (the thick strip at the bottom of the plug) until you can pass the cord under the collar. Each pin or blade will have a little screw that you should loosen until there is a gap big enough to take the copper wire. For a two-pin plug, simply twist the bare wires of each strand, put one into each pin hole, and retighten all the screws. For a three-blade plug, the procedure is a little more complicated because you must connect the colored strands to the correct blade. (The colors or the strands differ on old and new appliances.) The 'live' wire (brown or red) is always connected to the blade with the fuse, which is on the right-hand side of the plug as you look into it. The 'neutral' wire (blue or black) gets connected to the left-hand blade. Large appliances have a third 'earth' (ground) wire (green or green and yellow) that is connected to the top blade. Again, twist the copper wire ends and put them into the correct blade, then tighten all the screws. If you feel nervous or confused about doing this, either have someone show you the first time or undo a lamp plug and gaze at the mysteries inside first.

Food shopping

Whether you do your food shopping at a supermarket or a local shop, take your own shopping bag(s) with you because you will not be given anything to put your groceries in. Most food stores will *sell* you a plastic bag for about 5p, and they may also leave a few empty boxes around that you can take for free. However, most people take a substantial bag or basket or two-wheeled shopping cart with them. Small backpacks are also useful, as they save you from straining your arms.

Not only do you have to supply or pay for your shopping bag, but you also must pack your own groceries, even at supermarkets. This slows down the check-out procedure a great deal. Since groceries aren't always rung up in the order you want to pack them and there is usually little counter space to stack them on, the whole business is frustrating.

Avoid shopping for food on Monday mornings when stock is usually low. Saturday afternoons are extremely busy.

Labels on food are becoming increasingly informative, as there is growing pressure for manufacturers to reveal more about the ingredients, such as the quantity or percentage of each, the specific additives used, and some nutritional information.

Food for a picnic   If you are just buying food for a picnic, there are various places where you can get prepared foods. Bakeries often sell sandwiches as well as cakes and bread. Delicatessens and deli counters in the larger supermarkets have various sorts of sliced meats, cheeses, and salads. The food halls in Marks and Spencer stores carry a good range of packaged sandwiches, salads, cooked meats, cheeses, and fruit and desserts. Most grocery stores sell individual cartons of juice and even small bottles or cartons of wine, and beer can be bought by the can (even if the cans are displayed in four-packs).

Grocery stores   Grocery shops vary considerably in the kind and number of goods they sell, from very small mini-markets handling just the basics to huge supermarkets that carry impressive ranges of fresh, frozen, and tinned (canned) foods. The smaller the store, the less likely it is to sell fresh fruit and vegetables or much in the way of frozen goods. Most grocery shops do sell some beer and other alcohol, though. Even very small groceries may sell somewhat 'exotic' food if they are located in areas of ethnic diversity.

Many foods that seem familiar may be slightly different from what you are used to or come in smaller amounts (and often only the metric weight is given on the label). For example, some chicken stock cubes have caramel added to them (the English seem to like only dark-colored gravy); ham in tins (cans) is usually reconstituted and pressed; and tinned peas have an alarming green tint to them.

Some differences are in name only. Cookies and crackers are both called *biscuits* in England (sweet and savory, respectively). Potato chips are *crisps*; Jell-O is *jelly* and may come in gelatinous cubes rather than powder form; fish sticks are *fish fingers*; molasses is *treacle*; table napkins are *serviettes*.

English foods that are unfamiliar to most foreigners are numerous. Drinks include *Horlicks* (similar to Ovaltine), a malt drink served hot before bed; and *squash*, a fruit drink bought in concentrated bottled form and diluted at about four parts water to one part squash (flavors are orange, lemon, and lemon barley). Powdered custard mix makes a thick liquid custard (like unset vanilla pudding) that you serve on desserts. Frozen foods include *faggots* (port meatballs in gravy) and, believe it or not, *bubble and squeak* (Brussels sprouts or cabbage mixed with onions and potatoes and rolled into balls that are then covered with bread crumbs; it's not clear whether the name comes from the sound these make while they are cooking or from what they make you do after you eat them). There is a large variety of pickled vegetables: the sort called just *pickle* is a dark brown concoction made with mixed pickled vegetables and vinegar. But the real test of coping with English food is whether you can eat *Marmite*. This thick, dark brown yeasty paste is something you must be weaned on to like. Like the Australian version, Vegemite, it is spread on bread; when you first try it use it *very* sparingly.

Outside of London it is not always easy to find the more unusual kinds of foreign foods, although many large cities and towns will have a delicatessen, specialty food shop, or fancy supermarket that does carry some foreign goods. Health-food shops may also stock such items. (American foods that are difficult to come by include American-style hot dogs, lima beans, grape jelly, powdered ice tea mix, and root beer.)

Milk and milk products

Many people still have their milk delivered to their door every day, a wonderful convenience. To have milk delivered, try to catch a milkman near your house and ask him to call. Alternatively, look in the

Yellow Pages under 'dairies' and telephone to see if they cover your area. Payment is usually weekly (the milkman calls on a particular day to collect the money) or by a tokens system.

Milk is nearly all unhomogenized and mostly comes in small containers, from a half pint (10 ounces) to a quart. Low-fat and skimmed milk are on the increase in shops, but whole milk still predominates. You have a wide choice of the more fattening milk products: single cream, whipping cream, double cream, and even thick spreadable clotted cream are available. Soured cream and buttermilk are not as easy to find. All are fresh milk products.

There are also UHT (Ultra-Heat-Treated) milks, also called long-life milks, which have been treated in such a way that they keep on the shelf for six months or more. Once opened, they need to be put in the refrigerator like fresh milk. UHT milk is obviously very handy for camping, traveling, or just keeping on hand in case you run out of the fresh sort. However, UHT milks and creams do tend to have an aftertaste and are best used in cooking. UHT cream is often served with coffee in restaurants, so if you think the cream tastes funny, it may just be that it is UHT.

Milk and juice cartons were mainly designed by idiots. UHT and some juice cartons must be cut or torn open and then can't be properly closed up again. Whoever invented this type of container obviously never tried shaking an opened carton of orange juice or picking up a nearly full carton of UHT milk. Creams come in small yogurtlike containers with foil lids.

English cheeses are mainly mild and hard, although a few soft and stronger cheese have been created lately. Delicatessens and upmarket supermarkets will have the best selections. The better-known European cheeses can also be bought at most shops.

Butter comes in both salted and unsalted varieties.

English ice cream ought to be renamed, for much of it does not contain any cream. Most has vegetable fat in it instead (or worse, lard). If you want the real stuff, look for a label which says *dairy* ice cream.

Since Britain is a member of the EC, is relatively close to the Mediterranean countries, and has mild winters itself, there is a constant supply of good seasonal fresh fruits and vegetables. However, out-of-season, imported produce is quite expensive. (The word *produce* isn't often used in this sense in England except on supermarket signs.)

When at a greengrocery or a market stall, do not pick up things yourself. You must tell the clerk what you want, and he or she will weigh each purchase and put it into a little bag, which you in turn put into your shopping bag. The clerks will usually total the cost of your purchases in their heads.

Most fruits and vegetables sold in England are familiar to Westerners. The range of really exotic produce has been expanding lately though, as more and more English people travel to far-off places and as more people with different native cuisines settle in England. Native fruits include *conference* pears, which are hard and sweet, and varieties of apples such as *Cox*'s, which are eating apples, and *Bramleys*, which are soft, cooking apples. Strawberries and other berries (you can't find blueberries easily) are sold by the *punnet* (a small carton).

Some vegetables masquerade under what may be unfamiliar names: eggplant is called *aubergine* (pronounced 'oberzheen'), zucchini are *courgettes* ('kor-ZHETS'), rutabega is *swede*, and scallions are *spring onions*.

The most common lettuce is a soft-leaf one, similar to Boston lettuce, but other kinds of lettuce such as iceberg and Cos are on the increase. You ask for a lettuce, not a head of lettuce. Watercress, which has a spicy flavor to it, is widely available during warmer times of the year. You probably won't be able to find sweet potatoes, squash (the American kinds), or really good sweet corn.

Many greengrocers also sell cut flowers and potted plants.

Bakeries

Most neighborhood rows of shops include a bakery, but the supermarkets are also now expanding their bakery sections to include freshly made items.

Besides bread, bakeries always have a tantalizing display of sweet goods such as cakes, yeast doughnuts, buns, scones, tarts, etc., and of some savory items such as sausage rolls, small meat pies, and meat-filled pasties.

The breads that you are likely to find are white, whole wheat, wheat germ, granary (with coarsely milled bran), and bran loaves. These often can be bought sliced or unsliced. Dark breads such as rye or pumpernickel are mostly found at delicatessens. Bagels and cookies appear at some bakeries. Remember that bakeries are not generally open on Sundays (exceptions tend to be in London), and often run out of fresh bread by around 4 p.m. on weekdays.

English people don't usually buy decorated birthday cakes from bakeries. You do see some, but these are mostly fruitcakes. Wedding cakes, which *are* ordered from bakeries, are iced fruitcakes. (The English traditionally send slices of wedding cake through the mail in special boxes to people who can't attend the reception. A slice of cream-filled sponge cake would not survive such treatment, whereas fruitcake travels well.)

Butchers   England still abounds in old-fashioned butcher's shops, where the meat is not prepackaged and where you can tell the butcher to cut exactly what you want before your very eyes. Butchery is an art, and (unless you're a vegetarian) it is fascinating to watch a butcher deftly cutting chops or extracting bones from the meat. Some are so good that if you want a soup bone with a little meat on it, you have to ask for the meat separately, for the bone will be bare. Sometimes the fine cutting is still done on a wooden butcher's block, and there may even be sawdust on the floor. But there may also be gory sides of meat hanging from hooks in the shop, and unplucked pheasants and unskinned rabbits strung up during game season – not a pleasant sight for the squeamish. Cut meat is displayed in an open refrigerated counter.

Butchers also often sell cooked ham, meat pies, homemade pâté, sausages, and fresh eggs. They sometimes stock accompaniments such as mustard, horseradish sauce, stock cubes, and stuffing mix, as well as lard, beef dripping, and cheese.

The quality and cuts of English meat are somewhat different from those elsewhere. The beef can be very disappointing in flavor and tenderness, which is probably why the English cook it to death. If you want a cut of meat for a particular kind of dish, just explain to the butcher and he will recommend a cut. The following equivalents will help you in explaining:

Red meat

English	U.S.
fillet ('FILLit')	fillet mignon
braising steak	pot roast
rump steak	round steak
silver side and top side	rump roast
salt beef	corned beef
mince	hamburger

Lamb, which in fall and winter mostly comes from New Zealand, is excellent. Pork is also very good. Both lamb and pork chops sometimes have a slice of kidney left on them. Pork roasts come with ample skin and fat left on for crackling.

Ordinary bacon, which is either a back or a shoulder cut, comes in wide meaty strips, smoked or unsmoked. Streaky bacon has more fat in it and crisps up when cooked. Both kinds tend to be quite salty and often have rind on them. You can find bacon steaks at some butcher shops. English sausages are usually made of pork, but some have beef or even turkey in them. Most have thin skins and a mild flavor. Ordinary sausages are called *bangers* because they pop if you don't prick them before cooking; small sausages are known as *chipolatas*.

You can buy *offal* (kidney, liver, heart, tripe, etc.) at most butcher's shops. Calf liver is not as easy to find as pig or lamb liver.

Poultry comes in two kinds in England, battery or free-range, the difference being in the way it is raised. Battery fowl are cooped up in cages and fed a mixture

Poultry

of grain and fish meal, resulting in chicken or turkey meat that tastes of fish and lacks succulence. Free-range fowl, however, are allowed to roam and eat a variety of food and thus taste better and are juicier but are more expensive. If you cannot get free-range fowl, you'll probably be happier if you disguise the taste of the battery bird by cooking it in a heavily seasoned casserole. Chickens are cut into quarters at butcher's shops rather than into smaller segments.

The great turkey slaughter comes at Christmastime in England. Any other time of year, place your order a week or so ahead of schedule, as it may take a little while to convince the turkey to surrender early.

Game   Some butchers specialize in handling game (usually pheasant and rabbit), but most will be happy to order game meat for you if you ask well in advance.

Fishmongers   Not every row of neighborhood shops will have a fishmonger, but most large supermarkets stock some fresh fish or at least frozen fish. The closer to the coast you are, the more fish shops there will be. Fish is usually brought in fresh every day, which means that fish shops may be closed on Monday mornings since most fishermen rest on Sundays.

The types of fish available vary with the area and the season. Many kinds will be familiar to visitors: cod, haddock, herring, salmon, and trout. Less familiar types include Dover sole, lemon sole, plaice, and skate (all flat fish), coley, huss (dogfish), and whiting. Smoked fish is popular and readily available. You can also get delicacies like red mullet, squid, and roe.

Fish is sold whole and filleted (pronounced 'FIL-Litted'). Ask for half a fillet if a whole one is too much, and if you want the fish skinned, most fishmongers will do it for you.

The availability of shellfish depends on the season and the area. Shrimp are easy to get and are sold in the shell. (Note that what passes for a prawn in England couldn't be anything other than a shrimp in the U.S.) Other sorts of shellfish, like cockles, mussels, winkles, whelks (sea snails), and crab, are more often

found in marketplace stalls. You won't easily find
lobster or fresh oysters.

Hairdressers

There used to be a clear distinction between ladies'
hairdressers and men's barbers, but in recent years
unisex hair salons have become the norm (although
many older men still go to the barber's for a
traditional 'short-back-and-sides'). The names and
telephone numbers of hairdressing salons are listed in
the *Yellow Pages* and it is generally advisable to
telephone or go in to make an appointment (although
this is not always necessary). Most salons display
their prices. It is customary, but not essential, to give
a tip of around 10 percent.

**Laundro-
mats and
dry-cleaners**

For people who don't have laundry facilities at home,
there are laundromats (launderettes) in most suburban areas (not usually in town centers). If you plan
to use a launderette, arm yourself with a selection of
£1, 50p, 20p, and 10p coins to put into the automatic
washing machines and tumble dryers. It can cost
between £1.20 and £2 to wash and dry a load of
laundry. You can generally buy soap powder from a
vending machine on the premises, but taking your
own is cheaper. You will be expected to stay at the
launderette and do your washing and drying yourself
unless you ask the manageress to do a 'service wash'
for you, for an additional charge (not all launderettes
offer this service). Launderettes are often open till 10
p.m. and at weekends.

There are sometimes automatic dry-cleaning
machines at launderettes, but people usually take
their suits, skirts, coats etc., to a dry-cleaner's. These
are usually located in town centers or in suburban
shopping areas. Dry-cleaning services vary in speed,
price and quality but reputable chains such as
Sketchley and Bollom's are generally efficient and
reliable.

Public toilets

Almost all cities, towns, and large villages provide
public toilets. These are normally well signposted
(with the term *toilet* or *WC* or silhouettes of a man
and a woman). They are often near the central

shopping area; many older ones are located below ground. However, such toilets tend to be very cold and not very clean and rarely have hot water or enough toilet paper (if any). Many English women carry tissues if they are traveling and likely to need to use public toilets much – a sensible precaution. Toilets in large department stores and pubs are often more acceptable.

Public conveniences in England are nearly always free (with the exception of those in many train stations). Doors on the stalls go all the way down to the floor, making it harder for someone to steal things you've set on the floor.

The bewildering variety of flushing systems may confuse you at first. There are chains to pull, handles to push, round knobs on top of the cistern to pull up or press down, buttons on the wall to push in, and foot pedals to stomp on. As a general rule, whatever the device, press or pull long and hard.

Some toilets have automatic hand dryers that are activated simply by placing your hands inside what looks like a hole in the wall or under a nozzle. The hot air stops when you remove your hands.

Few public toilets offer areas for changing babies' nappies (diapers), although large department stores and motorway service stations are now including such facilities. There usually won't be anywhere set aside for nursing mothers, although women can breast-feed their babies in any public toilet (but there won't often be a chair to sit on while doing so in most). Women do not generally nurse babies in public in England.

Entertainment

One of the best places to find out what entertainment is available each day is in a local newspaper or local publication of events. These give information not only on movies and plays, but also about special exhibitions, festivals, concerts, lectures, and opening times for museums and stately homes. To find out what is going on in a larger area than that covered by the local press, look in the quality national papers (see p. 174) or visit the nearest Tourist Information Centre. You can also get a list of coming major events from the regional tourist authorities so that you can plan ahead of time. The monthly magazine *In Britain*, published by the British Tourist Authority, lists events all around the country for the month following that issue and gives highlights of that month's events. In London, the weekly publications *Time Out* and *What's On in London* give information about coming events and entertainment, as does the daily paper *The London Standard*.

The theater

Many tourists come to London specifically to go to the theater. For many people, the theater in England offers a wider choice of plays and is more affordable than theaters in their home countries (for example, tickets are currently about one-third the price of New York theater tickets). The range of plays and the quality of the productions is indeed very impressive. You can choose from serious drama, mysteries, comedies, and fringe (off-Broadway) performances and can always find a Shakespearean play to attend. Blockbuster musicals are so popular that it is difficult to get tickets for them.

Comedies and farces are silly in a way that only the English seem to be able to bring off, but the height of silliness and slapstick humor is the Christmas pantomime. If you are in the country near Christmas, you won't be able to escape this traditional form of entertainment. Pantomime plots are loosely based on children's stories and are embellished with singing, dancing, fairies, magical scenes, and moralizing. The male lead (the 'principal boy') is played by a woman, and the 'dame' is played by a man. Audience participation is essential – theatergoers are encouraged to shout set lines and hiss at the evil characters. It's all good fun, especially for children; and it is peculiarly British.

Don't think that good plays can be seen only in London or Stratford-upon-Avon. Most major cities and towns have very good provincial theater companies, producing both experimental and established works. You can even find open-air productions in the summer.

Getting tickets   You can always get a ticket for *some* show in London, since there are over 100 theaters of various sizes, but tickets for popular productions should be booked well in advance, especially for weekend performances. Tickets can be bought at theater box offices up to the time of the performance (if there are any left), but if you want to be assured of a good seat, plan ahead. You can reserve tickets over the phone – you will be asked to give a credit card number or to pick up and pay for the tickets at least a half hour before the show. Students with a valid student card can get half-price tickets at some theaters.

Theater tickets are also sold at some large London hotels and by ticket agencies listed in newspapers and the phone book (but are more expensive). Many such agencies are located along Shaftesbury Avenue. A good place to buy tickets is at the kiosk (booth) in Leicester Square, where spare tickets are half price on the day of the performance. The only drawback is that you may have to wait in a very long queue, and there is no guarantee you'll get tickets for the show you want to see the most.

Seating in theaters is either in the stalls (the ground-floor seats) or in the less expensive dress circle (balcony). There are a few boxes on the sides, but the viewing angle is usually not very good and certainly doesn't warrant the expense.

You do not need to dress up nowadays when going to the theater, especially for a matinee. People wear just about anything from jeans to dinner jackets.

Most evening shows start at 7:30 or 8 p.m.; matinees usually begin between 2 and 3 p.m. on Wednesday or Thursday and at 5 p.m. on Saturday. Theaters are not open on Sundays, unfortunately.

Many theaters are fairly old, and have interesting and beautiful architecture and decor. It is worth arriving early simply to look around. Smoking is not allowed inside the auditorium, so you'll have to do that before the performance as well. Programs must be bought from the ushers, but you do not have to tip them for pointing you to your seat.

It is customary to buy a small box of chocolates to eat during the performance so that you can disturb everyone else by rustling the paper during the quiet parts. At the interval (intermission), ushers sell ice cream and nonalcoholic drinks in the auditorium. You have to fight you way to the bar if you want an alcoholic drink at the interval. Many theaters have tried to alleviate this problem by allowing you to order and pay for your drink before the show starts – it will be waiting for you on a table at the interval.

Small binoculars are usually available for hire in each row of seats for 5 or 10 pence.

Ballet and opera

London has several good ballet companies, many of which are mainly touring companies. The emphasis remains on classical works, although contemporary dance is becoming increasingly popular. London bases for ballet performances include Covent Garden and Sadler's Wells.

Opera is gaining increasingly widespread appeal, no londer attracting only middle-aged, wealthy audiences. It is still the most expensive of the performing arts and tickets can be difficult to get for gala performances. However, in addition to London-based companies there are excellent touring companies such as the Welsh National Opera, and several small provincial companies. Tickets for productions outside London are less expensive, and there are sometimes stand-by discounts for students and unemployed people. One of the highlights of the opera season is the Glyndebourne International Festival Opera season, which runs from May through August. It's located in the rolling Sussex downs, set on the grounds of a Tudor mansion with an opera house attached to it. Opera-goers dress to the hilt, take a lavish picnic with them (there are expensive restaurants on the grounds), and relax on the immaculate lawns before and after the performances.

Music   Live music is well represented in England. There are many national, regional, local, BBC (British Broadcasting Corporation), and visiting orchestras of high quality that perform around the country and can also be heard live on the radio. Small chamber groups and soloists hold recitals in a variety of venues – churches, civic halls, stately homes, universities, etc. Classical choral music can be heard in religious and secular surroundings. Live classical music is one of the few types of entertainment you can find on a Sunday.

The BBC Promenade concerts in London, running from July through September, offer excellent performances of popular light classical works. The Proms – especially the last night – has become something of a cultural institution, with people of all ages queuing for hours outside the Albert Hall for standing room in the gallery. It is advisable to avoid the long (and sometimes fruitless) wait for tickets, however. A booklet containing the dates and programme for the forthcoming Proms can be bought from W H Smith and other bookshops and record shops during the spring.

Jazz clubs are not that numerous but are very popular. Live folk or rock music is performed at clubs, pubs, colleges, and the like and is usually advertised in the local press or on posters. Major rock bands come to the big cities, but the facilities in many towns (including university towns) are too small to attract the big groups. Tickets can be difficult to get for rock concerts, unless you buy far in advance.

Music and art festivals fill the summer calendar. They **Festivals**
include the huge Edinburgh Festival of Music and
Drama (in August and September), the Welsh
National and International Eisteddfodd (featuring
singing, poetry, prose, and dancing), the famous
Aldeburgh Music Festival, and an impressive variety
of music, art, and film festivals of various sizes. There
are also festivals devoted to beer, crafts, flowers,
Viking and Saxon culture, folklore, and rock music,
and shows for cats, dogs, horses, boats, cars, crafts,
antiques, and beer. A full list of dates and venues for
such festivals can be obtained from the British Tourist
Authority.

In England, one goes to the cinema (movies) – also **Cinemas**
known as the 'pictures' – to see a film. Watching films
used to be a much more popular form of entertainment, but now is fairly expensive. While the national
film syndicates distribute mostly current popular
films, smaller independent cinemas sometimes show
older films, foreign films, and documentaries. The
film ratings for admission age are: U – anyone; PG –
parental guidance suggested; 15 and 18 (minimum
ages).

Many cinemas still allow smoking inside, but it
may be restricted to one side of the auditorium. As in
the theater, the ushers sell ice cream at the interval
between movies. The popcorn that is sold at cinemas
is usually sprinkled with sugar, not salt.

Discos have cropped up in most large towns and **Nightlife**
cities; they tend to be crowded and very loud. Many
cater to young teenagers particularly, and you'll feel
out of place if you're not pretty trendy. For older
people, there are after-hours nightclubs which may
have dancing, but you often must be a member to get
in, although you can pay a fee and become an instant
member at many. There is a vast difference between
upmarket night clubs in big cities and the often rather
cozy clubs in provincial towns. Some London
nightclubs offer dinner and dancing, along with other
attractions such as gambling; again, most of these are
for members only, although posh clubs often have

reciprocal membership arrangements with equally posh clubs in other countries. Small comedy clubs provide entertainment along with refreshments.

Museums   In some ways all of England is a museum, full of historical monuments, prehistoric sites, Roman ruins, medieval churches and castles, old estate houses, etc. A sense of history permeates everything.

London has a very extensive range of excellent and famous museums, both general and specialized, large and small. They are usually easy to get to by public transportation. Most are free, although there may be a charge for special exhibitions; the Victoria and Albert Museum has just introduced voluntary charges. Most museums are open every day, from 10 a.m. to 6 p.m. on weekdays and from 2:30 p.m. to 5 or 6 p.m. on Sundays. Many museums do not allow you to take children around in push-chairs (strollers) or prams. After browsing through, you can buy items at the gift shop or refresh yourself with a drink and snack at those museums that have cafeterias. (Toilets are provided too.)

London isn't the only city with good museums. Most large cities and towns, and even smaller ones, have a few museums displaying local crafts, artifacts,

Reproduced by permission of *Punch*

art, etc. The museum buildings themselves are often of historical or architectural interest.

Stately homes are large estate houses that are or were lived in by the landed gentry and aristocracy. They attract both foreign and native tourists who want to see how the other half (1 percent really) lived. Stately homes often have wonderful collections of artwork, antiques, and furniture, as well as having beautiful grounds and gardens. They range from semi-ruined medieval castles to early twentieth-century houses, with a great variety of styles and sizes in between. The original owners have in many instances been forced to sell these houses because they can't afford the upkeep or because they have had to pay very high death duties when inheriting the property. So many of these stately homes have passed into the ownership and care of the National Trust, a private organization that also oversees various nature reserves, forests, and historical monuments in England.

Stately homes

Most stately homes charge an entrance fee for the house and grounds. (National Trust properties have free entry to members and it might be cheaper to obtain a year's membership if you intend to visit more than a dozen or so National Trust properties. You can join at most properties.) Some offer guided tours, while in others you are free to wander around on your own. There may be a small cafeteria or tea shop, and a gift shop at the site, and there will be toilets.

Visiting hours are quite unpredictable and depend largely on whether or not the house is still inhabited. An annual publication, *Historic Houses, Castles and Gardens* can be bought in major newsagents and gives opening times of all the major properties, both National Trust and private. Some are open all year round, every day, while others may be open only one or two days a week, or only on weekends and public holidays in the summer. Some allow tourists access only to the gardens. Closing time usually means the time you have to be out of the house, so you probably won't be admitted a half hour before that.

Churches   England is full of medieval churches that are interesting, well-preserved, and almost always free to visit.
The great cathedrals are beautiful, and are well worth
a visit. As well as seeing breathtaking examples of
English architecture, you may get to hear the choir or
the organist practicing. But remember that these
cathedrals are still in use, and you may be excluded
from certain parts during services. Some cathedrals
have gift shops selling guides and tasteful souvenirs.

Smaller churches in villages and towns are well
worth a visit too, not only for the beauty of the
buildings but also for the historical insights you can
glean from reading the plaques and stones in them.
Recently, however, many of these churches have had
to be locked between services because of vandalism.

Most churches have a collection box near the door,
and contributions from visitors are a vital source of
maintenance funds for smaller churches. Don't expect
to find toilets even at major city-centre churches.

Monuments   Other fascinating historical monuments, such as
Stonehenge, Hadrian's Wall, the ruins of numerous
abbeys, Roman ruins, etc., can be visited year-round.
(The National Trust owns many of these too. Others
are in the care of a government body called English
Heritage.) Some charge an entrance fee. There are
well over a thousand historic buildings scattered
throughout the country that are also open to the
public. If you plan to visit many sites, you can save
money on entrance fees by buying a season ticket to
the History of Britain, which will give you free
entrance to the major historical sites in the country.
Tickets are available from the Department of the
Environment, 25 Saville Row, London W1X 2BT.

Holidays and   In a land with such a long history and sense of
special   tradition, you would expect the natives to have
occasions   preserved a great many of the older celebrations and
to observe them enthusiastically. But except for royal
occasions, which are executed with great pomp and
flair, relatively little takes place on well-known
holidays, and a large number of traditional events
have all but died out. The English in fact don't go in

for much public celebration or festivity, seeming to prefer private or family gatherings to boisterous public displays. Perhaps this goes along with their general characteristic of not wanting to be seen to be too keen about anything.

Traditional local celebrations, though, are being revived and are well worth tracking down. These quaint and curious events include such celebrations as: cheese-rolling in Gloucestershire; Beating the Bounds (boundary markers) in London; Morris dancing displays by men wearing knee breeches, bells on their legs, flowered hats on their heads, and carrying staves; and a variety of local festivals (celebrating crab, cider, geese, medieval jousting, etc.). Any local tourist board will be able to inform you about such happenings in the area. *Traditional Britain* by Mark Martin (Golden Hart Guides, 1983) and *Bizarre Britain* by Roy Kerridge (Basil Blackwell, 1985) are good guides to such festivities, and events are also listed in the magazine *In Britain*.

The major national holidays and special occasions are given below with a brief description of the ways they are celebrated.

New Year's Eve

As in many other countries, people in England celebrate this by drinking themselves silly, making resolutions that they can't keep, and ringing in the new year at midnight by singing 'Auld Lang Syne.' In London the thing to do is to assemble at Trafalgar Square and watch people frolick illegally in the fountain, no matter how cold it is. In England and Wales, January 1 is a public holiday, giving everyone a day to sober up.

In parts of the north of England, as in parts of Wales and Scotland, people go 'first-footing' on New Year's Eve. This involves trying to be the first visitor of the year at a friend's or relative's house. You are supposed to bring some symbolic gift, such as a lump of coal, a piece of cake, a penny, or a bottle of whisky. After being fortified with drinks, people then move on to another house.

Lent

Shrove Tuesday, the beginning of Lent, is also known

as Fat Tuesday or Pancake Day, because the traditional way of celebrating is to stuff yourself with crêpes. In some places there still may be pancake races; in others, local variations of football (soccer), often with no rules, are attempted on the village green.

Mothering Sunday, the fourth Sunday of Lent, is the day that mothers are supposesd to receive cards, flowers, and attention from their children.

Maundy Thursday, the Thursday before Easter, is marked by the Queen's distribution of specially minted Maundy money to as many poor people as there are years in her life. This is a much more pleasant custom for her than the older one of washing poor people's feet.

Good Friday, the Friday before Easter, is a holiday. At breakfast everyone stuffs themselves with hot-cross buns – spiced sweet rolls with raisins inside, which are marked on the top with a cross.

Easter Sunday. Apart from the obvious church observances, this is mainly a family occasion, if celebrated at all. A few places still have an Easter parade, including London. Children may be given chocolate Easter eggs, but the custom of dyeing real eggs and searching for hidden eggs left by the Easter Hare seems to be dying out. Since school isn't in session for the week around Easter, this is also a time for fairs.

All Fools' Day (April 1)   Watch out on this day, for it is a time when people play tricks on each other. However, tricks are allowed only till noon. Don't believe what you read in the newspapers or hear on TV or radio on April 1, either (even after noon)!

May Day   May Day, the first Monday of the month, actually encompasses two different celebrations. The older, pagan version involves Maypole dancing, Morris dancing, and the selection of the May Queen. The modern version is in recognition of the worker and has strong socialist overtones. It is marked by rallies and speeches by politicians and trade unionists.

This popular event takes place on the second Sunday in June in London. It is in celebration of the Queen's official birthday (her real one is April 21, which isn't during the main tourist season). The Queen participates in a two-hour parade and takes the salute from her regiments. You don't actually have to go to London to see this, as, like most royal occasions, it is televised in its entirety. Tickets for the stands are very difficult to get, although it is not so hard to get in to see the rehearsals – but the Queen doesn't take part in these.

Trooping the Colour

Throughout the summer and early autumn there is an abundance of fairs, country shows, village fêtes, military tattoos (marching displays), steam engine rallies, and the like. Fairs usually have rides and games. Fêtes are smaller affairs, often held in the gardens of large houses or church grounds, and help raise money for good causes. They normally include stalls selling homemade food and crafts and have games.

Fêtes and fairs

The largest summer carnival is the Notting Hill Carnival put on by the West Indian community in London. There are floats, steel bands, and people in fancy costumes all letting themselves go – like a Mardi Gras in August.

Late September brings a few harvest festivals. Often this tradition survives only as a special church service.

Halloween is not traditionally celebrated in the southeast, although it is slowly creeping in there. Elsewhere, on October 31, children carve lanterns out of large swedes (rutabagas) or pumpkins, dress up in costumes, and hold parties. American-style trick-or-treating is not practiced, although some children are beginning to attempt to introduce it.

Halloween

A specifically English occasion, Guy Fawkes Night, on November 5, is a holiday celebrated with real enthusiasm. It commemorates the discovery of the Gunpowder Plot of 1605, when a man named Guy Fawkes tried to blow up Parliament and King James I.

Guy Fawkes Night

Today, an effigy of the man, called the 'guy,' burned on top of a large bonfire and fireworks are set off. For weeks beforehand, children drag these effigies around from house to house asking for 'a penny for the guy.' The money is supposedly used to pay for fireworks. In most towns a public firework display and bonfire are organized, and these draw large crowds. Otherwise many people have backyard parties. (Children are not allowed to buy fireworks, by the way.)

Opening of Parliament   This awesomely ceremonious occasion at the beginning of November is shown in all its glorious detail on TV. The Queen arrives at the Houses of Parliament in full regalia in a spectacular horse-drawn carriage. She then dons her royal robes and crown. A man called Black Rod leads her into the House of Lords (no monarch is allowed in the House of Commons). He then summons the members of the Commons after first suffering the indignity of having the door to the Commons slammed in his face. Once everyone is in the house of Lords, the Queen delivers a speech written by the government about the policies that her government will pursue in the next session. It is a colorful occasion, with the lords dressed in their ermine-trimmed robes and the bishops in full gear.

Christmas   Neither Christmas nor Easter are particularly religious holidays (see Religion, pp. 185–6). The main emphasis is on the family being together.

House decorations at Christmas are small and dignified – no pulsating lights or plastic Santas in the yard. The English prefer traditional garlands of holly and ivy, evergreen wreaths, and crepe paper and balloons. A small, uncluttered (often artificial) tree may be put up. Carol singers appear in shopping areas and go door to door, usually collecting money for charities.

On Christmas Day, children open the presents that Father Christmas has left in pillowcases that they've tied to the end of the bed. The Christmas meal usually centers on a turkey, which has replaced the more traditional goose. Seasonal goodies to follow include mince pies, Christmas pudding (a steamed, rich cake that is covered with brandy and set alight), and Christmas crackers (cardboard tubes that make a bang when pulled apart and are filled with a toy, a paper hat, and a silly saying or joke). In the afternoon, people relax around the TV to hear the Queen's message to the Commonwealth and have tea, which includes Christmas cake (a rich fruit cake covered in hard icing). Every English family has its own traditions in celebrating Christmas. You are really honoured if you are invited to join a family then.

Boxing Day (December 26) is the day when the tradesmen (postmen, milkmen, dustmen, etc.) traditionally were given their Christmas boxes (usually tips). Now it is a quiet family day, a time for outings if the weather is nice, or for watching football, getting together with relations (relatives) or friends, or just for recuperating from the previous day. Some towns hold Christmas fairs so you can freeze to death while getting sick on the rides.

In the past, many saints were honored by celebrations. Now only the patron saints of the U.K. countries are formally recognized, and very little celebrating goes on. Often the only clue to the fact that it is a patron saint's day is that TV news readers wear the national flower (a red rose for England, a daffodil for Wales, and a thistle for Scotland) and churches fly the national flag. Saint David, the patron saint of Wales, is honored on March 1, Saint George of England on April 23, and Saint Andrew, the Scottish saint, on November 30. Saint Patrick's Day (March 17), which is celebrated by Irish and non-Irish alike in the United States, comes and goes with hardly a notice in England except in areas with many Irish immigrants. Another saint who is remembered is Saint Valentine; on February 14 people send anonymous romantic cards to the secret object of their desires.

Saints' days

Sport and recreation

The English invented and developed many of the world's popular sports: soccer, cricket, tennis, rugby (from which American football has descended), rounders (from which baseball has evolved), snooker, squash, and a few others. Of these, cricket, soccer, and rugby are the most popular spectator sports. Unlike American sports events, and despite the English love of pomp and ceremony, major sporting occasions involve very few frills – the entertainment is in the game alone. There may be a brass or bagpipe band or a fife-and-drum corps playing before a game and at the interval, but these are fairly staid forms of entertainment. There are no cheerleaders – English fans are more than capable of cheering on their own at the right time without any external stimulus.

The national anthem is played only at international and championship games. Most people stand up for it, but many do not sing along. If they do sing, they often substitute 'God save our team' for 'God save the Queen.'

The English sense of fair play and good sportsmanship is legendary, and players still exhibit these virtues to a large degree. The same cannot always be said about the fans, though. But players and fans alike have had a hard time coming to terms with the fact that the English are no longer the best at most international sports, even those they invented.

Fans turn out in droves for professional sports, but do not watch school or university teams, who are supported by parents and a small number of other students. Fans are intensely loyal to their local teams, no matter how mediocre, and wouldn't dream of supporting a team from another part of the country.

Sports grounds of various sorts have a members' enclosure or pavilion, which requires appropriate

dress. Sometimes women are not allowed to sully this
area with their presence.

In England, the playing field is known as the *pitch*. **Terms**
Games are called *matches*, and a team's schedule for
the season is its *fixture list*. A *tie* refers to a match in a
knock-out competition. The championship match at
the end of a season is a *cup-final*.

When two teams end up with the same score, the
result is called a *draw* (except in cricket, where it is
called a *tie*). A *hat trick* means getting three of
something, as when one player scores three goals in
soccer.

Announcers give the name of the home team first
when reading the results. Teams are thought of as
plural entities, so they will say things like 'Liverpool
have beaten Chelsea' and 'England *are* all out.' Most
teams are not referred to by nicknames, but announcers do expect fans to know the names of all the
grounds where the teams play. Thus, if they say 'We
are now going over to White Hart Lane,' any soccer
fan will know that the home team is Tottenham
Hotspur (Spurs).

Sportspeople who have played on an international
team are said to have been *capped*, so someone who
has twenty caps for England has played in twenty
international matches.

Cricket is much loved throughout the British Com- **Cricket**
monwealth and little understood outside of it. The
important thing to remember is that cricket is a
civilized sport. It is meant to be played on a warm,
leisurely summer's day in an atmosphere of good
sportsmanship and dignity. The players, in their
dazzling white uniforms, look genteel and whole-
some. Spectators applaud politely when something
wonderfully exciting happens (though the fans have
been getting more boisterous of late). Cricket commentators, when not citing some of the endless
statistics surrounding the game – such as the most
runs scored by a fast bowler against Australia on a
Tuesday – tend to wax lyrical about the players, past
matches, the weather, or anything else that pops into

their heads. Play is stopped for lunch and tea. It is all jolly nice.

But what is an outsider to make of a game that can last for five days (yes, *five*); in which hundreds of points can be scored even though nothing seems to be happening much of the time; and which has a terminology all its own, like *silly mid-on*, *googly*, *night watchman*, and *having his eye in*?

Probably the best way for the uninitiated to follow a cricket match is to watch a game on television while listening to the radio commentary. At many cricket grounds, you are too far away from the action to be able to see in detail what is going on, although you can manage nicely with binoculars. Sitting in front of the TV, however, you will be able to observe play closely and clearly from a variety of angles and with the benefit of instant replay and slow-motion shots. The radio blow-by-blow account will help familiarize you with the terminology. After the basics become clear, which shouldn't take too long, then you can enjoy going to a match and soaking up the atmosphere.

The domestic cricket season runs from April to September; the national team tours abroad in the winter. In first-class cricket (see p. 156), play usually lasts for six hours a day – from 11:30 a.m. to 1:30 p.m., followed by a lunch break, then from 2:15 to 4:15 p.m., followed by a tea break, and from 4:30 to 6:30 p.m. You don't have to pay attention every minute; in fact, many people bring newspapers, crossword puzzles, and even knitting to the matches. On a good day, you can get a suntan. Food and beer are generally available at the grounds.

Basics   An understanding of baseball is very little help in understanding cricket. The teams do take turns at batting and fielding, runs are scored, balls are thrown to the batsmen, and batsmen can be caught out or run out, but cricket is slower paced, subtler, and more puzzling in its language than baseball.

The cricket field is generally oval in shape, about 175 yards across at the longest part. The boundaries are marked with white lines or rope. Approximately in the middle lies a strip of ground called the *wicket*, which is 22 yards long. There are three wooden *stumps* at each end of the wicket, which are put close enough together so that the ball can't pass between them. Two sticks called *bails* rest on top of the stumps. This collection of stumps and bails is also, perversely enough, called the *wicket*. A large white board known as the *sight screen* is placed at the boundary line behind each wicket in order to give the batsmen a plain background to see the red ball against.

Each team uses eleven players. There are fifteen people on the field at one time: the eleven players from the team that is fielding (not scoring points); two batsmen from the other team at bat (one at each end of the wicket); and two umpires (who wear what look like lab coats). The batsmen use flat, paddlelike bats and wear leg pads and gloves (and batting helmets if they know what is good for them) to

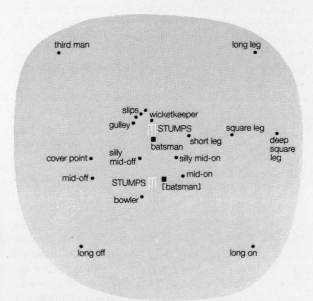

- player on the fielding team
- player on the batting team

A cricket pitch, showing fielding positions

protect themselves from the hard ball. The only fielder with heavier protective gear is the wicket-keeper, who is like the catcher in baseball.

The player who throws the ball is called the *bowler*. The batsman is trying to do two things: keep the ball from hitting the stumps behind him by hitting it away with his bat (he's out if he fails); and score runs by knocking the ball past the fielders to give him as much time as possible to run from one end of the wicket to the other. The fielders try to catch a ball that's been hit before it touches the ground or goes over the boundary rope.

Bowling   The bowler pitches six balls from one end of the wicket to the batsman at the other end. Then another bowler does the same from the other end to a second batsman. Each set of six balls is called an *over*. When an over is over, all the fielders change positions, since the ball will then be bowled and batted from the other end of the wicket. This helps to keep everyone awake.

The ball must be bowled straight-armed, with an over-arm motion. It is supposed to hit the ground in front of the batsman. There are many styles of bowling – fast and spin bowling are the most common. The bowler is basically trying to deceive the batsman about the path the ball will take when it bounces off the ground. Fast bowlers take a long run up to the bowling crease (line) in order to make the ball go faster and try to make the ball curve in the air. Spin bowlers usually take only a few steps before pitching the ball. They rely on different grips and spins when releasing the ball to make it 'break' at various angles after hitting the ground. If a ball doesn't hit the ground before reaching the batsman, it is called a *full toss*. Such balls are easy to hit.

The bowlers rub sweat and spit on the ball and polish one side of it on their legs in order to affect the flight of the ball. This is perfectly legal, but leaves a nasty red smear on their dazzling white trousers.

The style of bowling used depends on many things, such as whether the batsman is right- or left-handed; the condition of the wicket (whether the ground is hard or soft, even or rough, etc., which determines how fast and how much the ball will bounce); and how new the ball is (newer balls are 'livelier'). If a ball goes into the crowd, it must be returned, since the condition of the ball affects the bowling a great deal.

Fielders may stop the ball with any part of their body, including their feet. Fielding positions are determined by the type of bowler, batsman, and general game strategy. An attacking field is one in which most of the fielders are close in to the batsmen. It may look like the fielders just stand around enjoying the weather most of the time, but in fact they have the difficult job of concentrating on the play for hours at a time. The wicketkeeper's job is especially demanding.

Fielding

The fielding positions must have been named by someone who had too many beers on a hot summer's day (see diagram). The *off* side of the field is the side towards which the batsman's bat points; the other side is called the *on* or *leg* side.

For a team to score a run, the two batsmen must exchange places after the ball is hit and before a fielder knocks the bails off the stumps with the ball. The batsmen carry their bats when they run and are deemed safe at the other end of the wicket when the bat has crossed the line at that end. They run back and forth as many times as they can, scoring one run every time they exchange ends.

Scoring

If a batsman hits the ball so that it crosses the boundary rope before touching the ground, he automatically scores six runs. If the ball touches the ground and then travels over the boundary, he has four runs (both *fours* and *sixes* are called *boundaries*). Unlike in baseball, the batsmen do not *have* to run when the ball is hit if they don't think they can safely make it to the other end. Sometimes a batsman will just hit the ball gently to keep it away from his stumps, with no intention of scoring runs. There is no penalty for swinging at the ball and missing, as long as the ball doesn't hit the stumps - only embarrassment.

A team can also score runs from *extras*, which are errors by the fielders. The types of extras are:

no ball: a ball that is bowled illegally (usually because the bowler has stepped over the bowling line or has bent his arm); worth one run.

wide: a ball bowled so high or wide that the batsman couldn't possibly have hit it; worth one run, or four if the ball crosses the boundary.

bye: a ball that the batsman hasn't hit but which has not been stopped by the wicketkeeper or fielders; worth as many runs as the batsmen can make.

leg bye: a ball that glances off the batsman's body and isn't stopped by the fielders (the batsman can't do this on purpose); worth as many runs as the batsmen can make.

A batsman who makes 100 runs on his own batting is said to have scored a *century*, a noteworthy feat. If no runs are scored in an over, the bowler is credited with bowling a *maiden over*.

Outs   One team stays at bat until it has lost ten wickets, that is, until ten of their eleven men are out. If a team has four wickets *in hand*, this means that it has four men *not* out, and thus has lost six of its ten wickets. If the announcer says the team is '134 for 2,' that means it has scored 134 runs and lost 2 wickets.

There are ten ways in which a batsman can be out, thus ending his time at bat, but four are most common:

bowled: when the bowler hits the stumps with the ball, causing the bails to fly off.

caught: when a fielder catches the ball the batsman hit before it touches the ground. After making a catch, the fielder hurls the ball high into the air in an unrestrained show of elation.

run out: when the batsmen are trying for a run but a fielder knocks the bails off the stumps (by throwing the ball at the stumps or pushing the bails off with the ball in his hand) before the batsman safely crosses the line in front of those stumps.

leg before wicket (LBW): when a batsman uses his body to stop a ball which, in the opinion of the umpire, would have hit the stumps. This is very difficult to judge, due to the speed of the ball, the angles at which the ball can come off the ground, and the fact that the batsman is partially blocking the umpire's view of the stumps. Fielders who think that a batsman is guilty of LBW jump in the air and shout something like 'How's that?' (the only sort of appeal one is allowed to address to an umpire). The umpire may take a long time to decide this, because he has to mentally calculate the line of the ball. If he does decide the batsman is guilty of LBW, he raises the index finger of one hand.

Reading a scoreboard

Scoreboards are laid out differently at the various grounds, but they all display so many numbers that it is almost impossible to figure out what they all mean. At the top of the board is the number of runs scored. Beneath that will usually be the number of wickets lost (outs); who the current batsmen are; and individual batsmen's totals. After that may come how many runs the last batsman made, how he got out, the number of overs bowled by each bowler, how many runs there were when each wicket fell, and the number of extras scored.

Levels of play and strategy

International matches, called test matches, start on a Thursday and last for five days (with no play on Sunday). In London, they are played at Lord's and the Oval cricket grounds. Each team is allowed two *innings*, or turns at bat. However, sometimes one team hasn't completed their second innings by the end of the fifth day. In that case, the game ends in a *draw*, which means that no one wins, even if the first team was ahead by 200 runs. A team that knows that it cannot win the match will try to play for a draw by having the batsmen bat cautiously to prevent getting out and not worry about making runs. If a team is leading by a huge margin and has been at bat so long that the other team might not get to complete its second innings, it will often *declare* its innings closed – that is, quit batting before all ten men are out. A team that has just batted but did poorly and is 200 or more runs behind the opponent may be made to *follow on* (bat again immediately), which lessens the chance of a draw and saves the other team's energy.

The top professional cricket clubs represent counties. There are seventeen clubs playing 'first-class' cricket. Other counties have teams, but play in a 'minor counties' league. First-class matches last three days, with each team having two innings. There are also one-day limited-over matches, where play is restricted to 40 to 60 overs bowled per team. Thus, the second team gets to bat even if the first team is not all out. The strategy in one-day matches is different from that in full first-class cricket matches in that the emphasis is on scoring runs more than on taking wickets. There is more action, but there is also less subtlety and variety to the run of play. True cricket lovers scorn the one-day matches.

Sportsman-ship Part of the appeal of cricket is the sporting way in which it is played. No one argues with the umpire or calls into question his eyesight, neutrality, or intelligence. Even commentators won't say a call was wrong when the instant replay clearly shows that it was. Fielders don't pretend that they have caught a ball when they haven't. And if a batsman has just snicked (touched) a ball that is caught behind him, he doesn't wait to see if the umpire noticed – he simply walks off the field. Poor sportsmanship just 'isn't cricket.'

Soccer Soccer is known in England as *football*, which is short for Association Football, the game's official name. Football is best thought of as a predominantly male, working-class religion that is practiced on Saturday afternoons from 3 to 4:45, from mid-August to mid-May. It is by far the most popular sport in England, both in terms of the number of professional and amateur teams and the number of spectators, and so gets very heavy media coverage. Soccer is also one of the most popular sports in the world, and international competitions are an important part of the sporting year for English soccer fans.

The English Football League (now named after a

sponsoring company each year) consists of ninety-two clubs from all over England and Wales. It is amazing to think that such a small country can actively support so many clubs. In fact, many teams are now in financial trouble.

The teams are divided among four divisions according to how good they are, with the First Division being the best. Each team plays the others in its own division twice during the season. Teams are awarded three points for a win and one for a draw. At the end of the season, the teams with the highest number of points at the top of the First Division go on to some special competitions the following season. Each league division champion gets a trophy. In addition, the top teams in the Second, Third, and Fourth divisions are promoted into the next higher division, while the bottom ones of each division get relegated. This all adds spice to the matches at the end of the season.

There are various knock-out competitions during the season in which all the divisions and even some nonleague teams participate. These end in cup-final games at Wembley Stadium in London.

The Scots have a separate football league consisting of the premier division (ten teams), and the first and second divisions (fourteen teams each). Scotland, England, and Wales each have national teams that play in the international competitions.

If you want to go to a football match, you can just turn up at the ground before a match and buy a ticket or pay at the gate. For very popular teams, it is best to buy a ticket a few days in advance at the club's ticket office. *Going to a match*

You usually have a choice of paying either for a seat of for the dubious but less expensive pleasure of standing up for an hour and three-quarters on the terraces among the more vocal fans. Children who have to stand often bring a box or stool to stand on so that they can see.

Almost all matches are played on grass. No ground is entirely under cover, so if it rains, the players slide around in the mud and the spectators in the front stands get wet. Grounds of lower-division teams may have only the seated section covered, or may not have any seating at all.

Fans'
behavior
Much publicity has been devoted lately to the English 'football hooligans' who go to matches solely, it seems, to fight with rival fans or with each other. It must be stressed that such idiots are in a minority, and are often more in evidence at international matches than at domestic ones. The best way to avoid any unpleasantness is to stay away from the terrace end where the visiting supporters are located. You will normally be perfectly safe anyway unless you are a young male who looks aggressive and is wearing one team's colors. The teams whose so-called supporters have the biggest reputation for causing trouble are Chelsea and Millwall (in London), Leeds, and Manchester United, though these are not the only ones.

For the most part, English soccer fans are spirited but well behaved. Spontaneous chanting and singing constantly break out from the terraces during matches. You might not want to strain too hard to catch all the words, since some chants are rather obscene. Fans also wave scarves and banners with their team's colors. Disapproval is signaled by whistling.

Style of play
Different countries have developed their own styles of playing soccer. English teams tend to play at a faster pace than many others. They are certainly more aggressive than North American soccer players, without necessarily being nasty. But you find few players with the tremendous ball-control skills of many Continental and South American teams. Most English teams seem to move the ball down the field by kicking it in the air rather than by dribbling or passing the ball.

Rules
Most people around the world are familiar to some degree with how soccer is played, but for those who are totally ignorant of the rules, the following is a brief guide to the major points of play.

The game is played by two teams of eleven players each, with one substitution allowed. One referee and two linesmen control the match. Play is continuous over two 45-minute periods. The aim is to score *goals* (points) by getting the ball into the opponent's net (one point each time). Only the goalkeeper is allowed to touch the ball with his hands, and only shoulder-to-shoulder contact is allowed between players.

When a player knocks the ball *into touch* (over the side line), someone from the other team throws the ball back into play. If he knocks the ball over the boundary line at his opponents' end of the pitch, the opponents' goalkeeper puts the ball back into play with a *goal kick*. If he knocks it over his own end line, the other team is given a *corner* – it gets to kick the ball from the corner near where the ball went out.

A *free kick* is given to the opposing team when a player commits some foul, is offside, or exhibits unsportsmanlike conduct (including arguing with the referee). However, the referee can *play advantage* and not stop for the foul if the team that would get the free kick has the run of play going its way at that moment. Players can be booked or warned for serious fouls. If a player commits two serious fouls, he is sent off the field and cannot be replaced. Note that contrary to North American usage, a foul *on* a player means that that player did not commit the foul, but was fouled *by* someone else. A player is *offside* if there aren't at least two opponents between him and the other team's goal when one of his teammates passes the ball forward.

One soccer term that is widely used outside of the game is *own goal*. You score an own goal by hitting the ball into your own net, thus giving the opponent a point. In essence, it means you have shot yourself in the foot.

Rugby

Rugby, known to its supporters as 'rugger,' is a much more physical game than soccer. There are two distinct branches of the game. *Rugby Union*, the original version, has amateur status, so players aren't paid for their efforts. This means they are either totally obsessed with the game or else are independently wealthy, or both. In England, Rugby Union has upperclass overtones – it is taught in private boys' schools, where it is thought that rough sports are good for building character. In Wales the game is working-class and is seen by many as their national sport. There are few more moving spectacles than being in a rugby stadium packed with Welshmen when they sing 'Land of My Fathers' in three-part harmony. *Rugby League* is the professional version of the sport. It is played mainly in the north of England by working-class men.

The rugby season runs from October through April. The major Rugby Union tournaments are staged at Twickenham in London, while the Rugby League cup-final is played at Wembley. International matches are played throughout the season.

Union rules Rugby Union is played by two teams of fifteen players and two substitutes. One referee and two linesmen keep the game under control. The game is mainly continuous, and is played over two 40-minute halves. The pitch is 110 yards long, with a set of H-shaped goalposts at either end. The ball is oval in shape.

Players can kick, pass, or run with the ball. The aim is to score *tries* and *goals*. A *try* is given when a player carries the ball over his opponent's goal line and touches the ball to the ground; it is worth 4 points. A *goal* is scored when the ball is kicked between the goalposts, over the crossbar. There are three types of goal: a *conversion* after a try, worth 2 points, which is taken from a spot about 15 yards from the goal line in line with where the ball was touched down; a *drop-kick*, when the ball is dropped to the ground and kicked on the rebound, worth 3 points; and a *penalty kick*, worth 3 points. No points are awarded for a *touch down*, which is when a player grounds the ball in his own goal area; play is restarted either with a drop-kick or a *scrum* (see below), depending on who made the ball go into the goal area.

Players cannot pass the ball forward, but there is no limit on the number of sideways passes they can make. The ball can be kicked forward, and any player can catch it or pick it up. A player who catches a ball kicked by an opponent can yell 'Mark' and get a free kick from that spot. Often a ball is kicked *into touch* (over the sideline) so that the team can gain ground through a *line-out* (see below).

Only the player with the ball can be tackled. Players wear minimal protective gear (shin pads and teeth guards), so it is important that tackling isn't done in a vicious manner. (Even so, bloody noses occur.) As soon as the ball carrier is on the ground, he must let go of the ball and the tackler must let go of him. Anyone not on the ground can then play the ball. In reality, there is usually a pileup before the ball gets free. Quite often players try to rip the ball from the carrier's hands rather than tackle him. To keep from being tackled, the ball carrier is allowed to *hand off* – push the tackler away with a stiff arm. A tackled player can score a try if his momentum carries him across the goal line.

A *scrum* is used to restart play after certain infringements of the rules. It is a cross between a huddle and a shoving match and resembles a huge spider with an extra set of legs. Eight players from each team face the same direction and form an interlocked bunch with three players at the front; the two bunches then join up to create a tunnel between them. The ball is thrown into the tunnel by the *scrum half*. The *hooker*, who is the middle player in the front of each bunch, tries to heel the ball back through the *pack*, who heel it out of the scrum where it can be picked up by one of their teammates. It is illegal – and highly dangerous – to make the scrum collapse.

When the ball goes into touch, play is restarted with a *line-out*: the teams form two parallel lines at a right angle to where the ball went out of bounds. A player then throws the ball straight between the two lines of players, who try to get control of the ball. If a ball goes out of play beyond the goal line, the team defending the goal gets to drop-kick the ball away from within their 25-yard line.

A player is *offside* if he is in front of a teammate who has the ball or who last touched the ball. When in an offside position, a player cannot touch the ball or interfere with an opponent, which is why it sometimes looks like players are just standing around doing nothing.

League rules   Rugby League is similar to Union in many respects. It is rougher, though (it is not uncommon to see a tackler push the tacklee's face into the ground as they try to get up). Differences involve several aspects of the game. For instance, in Rugby League, teams get only 2 points for a penalty kick and 1 point for a drop goal. There are fewer players on a team (thirteen), and usually only six participate in a scrum. There are no line-outs; instead, a scrum is formed where the ball went into touch. A major difference is in what happens after a tackle. In Rugby League, the tackler must let the tackled ball carrier get up immediately; the tackled player then heels the ball back to a teammate. The team with the ball is allowed five successive tackles and restarts; on the sixth tackle, a scrum takes place.

Other sports   There are, of course, a large variety of other sports played professionally and enjoyed by amateurs throughout England. Many get good coverage in the media.

Horse racing   Horse racing is very popular, especially because off-course betting is legal. Television covers all the betting odds for those who have a keen financial interest in the races. Even radio news announcers give tips on the horses. Newspapers list racing venues and betting odds.

The flat-racing season goes from the end of March to early November. There are many notable races, the best known being the Derby (pronounced 'Darby'), which takes place in the first week of June at Epsom, south of London. Royal Ascot occurs over four days in the third week of June and is located to the southwest of London. Royal Ascot is not just a series of horse races – it is also an upper-class fashion show. Men in the Royal Enclosure must wear top hats and tailcoats and the women wear frilly dresses and fancy hats. The Royals arrive in horse-drawn carriages.

The steeplechasing season (hurdles and jumps) goes on for most of the year, excluding June and July. The two best-known steeplechase races are in March: the National Hunt Festival in Cheltenham and the Grand National in Liverpool. The latter is an endurance test – forty horses race 4 1/2 miles over thirty jumps - and few actually finish.

Show-jumping and dressage riders wear formal coats and jodhpurs and black hats as they guide their horses through their paces. The Badminton Horse Trials in April is a popular event, combining show jumping, dressage, and cross-country riding, while the culmination of the season is the Horse of the Year Show in London in October. *Showjumping*

Polo is another horsey sport that is mainly played by the upper classes, largely because of the expense of owning your own horse. Prince Charles is a keen polo player. The sport is a sort of hockey on horseback, with four riders per side playing for eight short periods called chukkers (or chukkas). *Polo*

Greyhound racing is popular, especially among the working classes, and can be seen mainly in London. The dogs chase an electrified hare around the track. Betting is similar to and as fierce as that in horse racing. *Dog racing*

For the last week of June and the first week of July, the grass-court tennis competition at Wimbledon in London captures the attention of nearly everyone in England (and of many around the world). If the weather is fine, people flock to sit in the sun, eat strawberries, and watch the stars battle it out. *Tennis*

If you want a seat at one of the show courts (center court and court number 1), you must apply at least six months in advance to The Chief Executive of the All England Lawn Tennis and Croquet Club, P.O. Box 98, Church Road, London SW19 5AE. Tickets are assigned by lottery, so you may not get one even after sending in for it. You can stand in line all night for a standing-room ticket at the main courts; or, if you're lucky and a ticket holder leaves early, you can buy that ticket cheaply. If you're not particular about which tennis players you watch, just pay the general entrance fee (half price after 5 p.m.) and watch whomever you can. At the beginning of the tournament you can still see top players on the outside courts.

Other major tennis tournaments are held in England throughout the year, indoors (there is even one staged at the Albert Hall) and out. They don't seem to attract as much interest as Wimbledon, though.

Snooker   Snooker (which rhymes with *lucre*, not *cooker*) was invented in India by British officers who didn't have anything better to do. However, today a talent for the game is seen as a sign of a misspent youth. At the professional level, it is an appealingly genteel sport, with the players dressed neatly in waistcoats and ties. The referee wears white gloves, and the audience is usually quiet and restrained.

Snooker is a close cousin of pool but is played on a larger table. There are fifteen red balls, each worth 1 point, and one each of six other colored balls worth differing points: yellow (2), green (3), brown (4), blue (5), pink (6), and black (7). The aim is to get the most points by potting (knocking) the balls into the six pockets using a wooden cue stick and a white cue ball. The balls must be potted in a certain order: first a red, then a color, then a red, and so on. When a colored ball is potted, it is returned to the table to an assigned spot until all the red balls have been put in. Then the colored ones must be potted in the order of their value, ending with the black.

Players get another shot every time they pot a ball. If they hit or pot the wrong ball, the opponent is given penalty points. One playing strategy is to *snooker* the opponent by leaving the white ball in such a position that the opponent can't get a clear shot at the ball he is supposed to hit. (From this comes the English term *snookered*, meaning 'in a difficult position.')

A *break* is a series of uninterrupted shots by one

player. The maximum number of points a player can score from a break is 147, a very rare event.

Darts is played in most pubs throughout the country. It is also played at the professional level and is often televised. The contestants hardly look like athletes, usually sporting beer bellies and smoking and drinking during the match.

The circular dart board is divided into twenty wedges, which are numbered in what seems to be haphazard order. Each wedge has four bands: the thin outer band is worth twice the wedge number; the thin inner band is worth three times the wedge number; and the two broader sections are worth the number on the wedge. The circular bull's-eye in the middle has two bands, the outer worth 25 points and the inner 50.

Each player starts with 501 points (301 in pub darts). A turn consists of throwing three darts. The points made on each turn are subtracted from the total. The first player to reach 0 exactly wins, but the last dart must land on an outside (double value) band. In pub darts, you must also start on a double value band.

Bowls is a very old game (dating from around the thirteenth century) and is popular mainly with older men and women. It is played outdoors on immaculate, closely mown grass greens or indoors on carpeted greens.

One player rolls a small white ball (the *jack*) out to the far end of the green. Then two players take turns rolling four balls each toward the jack. The balls are weighted to make them curve when rolled at slower speeds. The object is to score points by getting the most bowls closest the the jack. It is perfectly within the rules to knock opponents' bowls out of the way.

There are a host of other sports enjoyed in England on both professional and amateur levels. Golf, which was invented in Scotland, is very popular, and several professional tournaments are held each year. There are competitive leagues for field hockey for men and women. Badminton, squash, and table tennis tournaments are also held. World-class speedway and motorcycle riders compete through clubs.

A popular women's sport is netball, which is similar to basketball except that players can pass the ball only in the air. Men's basketball teams are springing up around England, and games are even televised occasionally.

Amateur rowing clubs are fairly common. The Henley Regatta, which takes place on the first Thursday through Sunday in July, and the annual Oxford and Cambridge boat race in March are highlights of the rowing season. In August, there are sailing races around the Isle of Wight. Power-boat racing events take place in certain docks, e.g., in Bristol.

Recreation For those who would rather participate in sport than watch it, England offers many good facilities. Golfers can use the public golf courses, which can be found near most towns. Some hotels offer entrance to private golf courses, and you can often arrange to use a private course on a weekday, for a fee. You may have to join a club to get a game of badminton or squash, but public tennis courts are sometimes located in public parks. Ask in the local tourist office to find out what is available.

There are a few public ice-skating rinks scattered about the country, and some roller-skating rinks. Skiing is possible in Scotland if the weather cooperates.

Swimming Most large cities have at least one swimming pool, which is often called the *public baths* (not to be confused with real spa-type baths found in some places). Most hotels don't have one. You can also swim in the sea and in lakes, depending on the time of year. On the south coast, you can sunbathe in May, but the water might not be warm enough for most people until June or July; it usually stays tolerable through September. The North Sea and the sea off Scotland warm up more slowly than the Channel, so July may be the earliest to swim there comfortably. Hardy people do swim at other times of the year.

Some of the most beautiful, undeveloped, and secluded beaches in England are hard to get to or far from big cities. The more accessible beaches are over-used and are often surrounded by resorts, bingo halls, arcades, and amusement piers. All beaches are free, and everyone has access to the beach below the high-tide mark, night or day.

Popular beaches may have a public toilet and a food or ice cream stall nearby. However, there won't be anywhere to change clothes. Most people change on the beach with a towel wrapped around them for modesty. Few people sunbathe in the nude (it isn't legal), but women in topless suits are increasingly tolerated, especially on parts of Brighton beach.

At the more popular beaches you can rent deck chairs, and sometimes sun umbrellas as well. To protect balding heads from the sun, men often cover their pates with a handkerchief whose corners have been knotted – the height of beach fashion! At popular locations you may also find tiny beach huts for rent which provide a place to change and get out of the sun; some even have an electric plate for making tea. At other places you may just have to huddle behind a canvas windbreak.

Dangers to beware of on the English coasts include small jellyfish, which give a mild but irritating sting, and crumbly chalk cliffs. There aren't usually any lifeguards at the beaches, so be careful to note when the tide is supposed to go out, and look out for cross currents (there are usually signs posted at dangerous spots). If there is a red flag flying, don't swim.

Watersports

Sailing is very popular in England, ranging from dinghies used on any lake or river large enough, to the ocean-going yachts of the very wealthy. Organized trips/lessons can easily be found. Sailing is permitted on many reservoirs, but you may have to join a club.

Rowing boats can often be hired by the hour at popular tourist spots on rivers or lakes. For the venturesome, the famous punts (flat-bottomed boats propelled by plunging a long pole to the bottom of the river and leaning on it) of Oxford and Cambridge can be hired for trips along the rivers.

Keen waterskiers will find the Lake District in summer very attractive.

Windsurfing is becoming very popular on inland waterways and disused gravel pits that have been filled with water. You can easily rent boards in many places. If you're very adventurous, you can even surf off the Cornish coast.

Rock climbing   Many areas of England are ideal for rock climbers. People interested in potholing (caving) can also find places in which to follow this urge. There are clubs that organize both activities.

Riding   Pony trekking and horse riding are fairly expensive outdoor pursuits, but again they are not difficult to find in country areas. Many riding stables offer lessons or group rides, as well as simply renting out riding horses.

Bird watching   Most rural and coastal areas of England are excellent for bird watching. The variety of habitats makes for a rich assortment of bird life, which is supplemented by migrants. Conservation organizations provide access to bird blinds (sometimes for a fee) at bird sanctuaries.

Cycling   See pp. 63–4.

Blood sports   England has much to offer those people who enjoy killing animals. Such activities are called field sports.

The fox-hunting season runs from about November to April. Upper-class riders in full ceremonial gear with packs of hounds (they are never referred to as mere 'dogs') charge over fields after a petrified defenseless fox ('the unspeakable in full pursuit of the uneatable'). If the fox is caught, the hounds rip it to pieces. Don't count on being invited to join a hunt unless you have connections, for they are quite exclusive occasions. Of late, hunt saboteurs have tried to stop fox hunting by various nonviolent means. Some enlightened hunters now lay a scented trail for the hounds to follow, rather than have them pursue a red fox, whose numbers are dwindling.

Hare coursing (September to March) is also popular with the upper classes. This sport pits dog against hare. The hare is given an 80-yard start, then two greyhounds (or similar breeds) race each other to see which can get to the hare first, quite often killing it in the process. The Waterloo Cup is the highlight of the coursing season.

Visitors are allowed to go shooting in England, with proper gun and game-killing licenses (which you can get, respectively, at the main police station and the post office in the area). Or you can go on an organized shoot, with guide and gear provided, at great expense. You cannot shoot wherever you please, but need the landowner's permission to shoot on his or her property. There are also defined hunting seasons for protected species. Deer-stalking season varies with the region and type of deer. Grouse season opens on August 12 (known as 'the glorious 12th'), partridge and wild fowl season in September, and pheasant season in October. Bird-hunting seasons generally end at the beginning of February.

By far the most popular blood sport in England is angling. Fishing from the beach is free and is popular year round, no matter what the weather. You can hire boats for sea fishing, and you may even be able to persuade a local fisherman to take you on board. However, fresh-water fishing, which is divided into game fishing (salmon and trout) and coarse fishing (other fish), is rarely free. Most river banks and fishing rights for lakes are owned by clubs or individuals, so you need to have a rod license (from the local tackle shop) as well as permission to fish that particular stretch of water. Hotels near lakes and rivers often can arrange for fishing for guests.

Fishing

For information on specific recretional activities, write to the British Tourist Authority (see Appendix), which will send you booklets with details of facilities around the country. In addition, once in Britain you'll find many popular magazines devoted to particular pastimes.

The media

Television   The quality and variety of programs on English TV (widely known as 'the box' or 'the telly') is generally very impressive. The very high level of video-recorder ownership and rental in England attests to this, as they are mainly used to tape TV programs rather than to watch rented movies.

Programs   British documentaries and wildlife programs are excellent. Serialized adaptations of novels also tend to be very good. Situation comedies are mainly good, and at least do not usually continue past the point of exhaustion (some are kept on for only six or thirteen episodes). Comedy variety shows are ... well ... very English. They often rely on old jokes, suggestive remarks, and transvestitism for humor, which is not to say that they aren't sometimes very funny. Many of the newer-style comedy shows hit the heights (or depths) of sarcastic humor. Some quiz shows are very English, with very knowledgeable and quite restrained contestants and no prizes awarded. Sometimes the contestants are all celebrities and the score is incidental. However, more of the inane, American-style quiz shows are invading the screen nowadays.

National news programs vary in length and degree of bias toward the Establishment. Most are factual rather than chatty, with the noted exception of breakfast-time news shows and some local news programs. The weather report always comes at the end of the program. Most news announcers have an accent that is generally easy for foreigners to understand.

There is no official censorship, although you won't see many 'video nasties' on TV. You will see naked breasts and bums (bottoms) and hear some obscene words, though.

There are four TV channels, all of which are *Channels*
broadcast nationwide. The British Broadcasting Corporation (BBC) runs two noncommercial channels,
BBC 1 and BBC 2. These are financed partially
through yearly TV license fees. (Yes, you have to buy
a license for your TV from the Post Office, just as if it
were a dog, even if you just rent your set. Detector
vans drive around picking up TV signals and checking
to see if the house from which each signal is coming
has paid up. Fines for not having a license can run to
several hundred pounds.) The other two stations,
Independent TV (ITV) and Channel 4, raise money
through commercial advertising. Some effort has been
made to introduce cable TV, but so far only a few
small areas have been hooked up.

BBC 1 carries mainstream, general-interest programs.   *BBC*
It has things like a breakfast-time news/chat show,
children's shows during the day, local and national
news, some live sports, movies (with no breaks – so
be prepared to sit still for the duration), popular series
(including some American ones), chat (talk) shows,
current affairs, documentaries, plays, and so on.
    BBC 2 also carries mainstream programs and live
sports, but tries to cater to more highbrow tastes. It
shows school programs in the mornings; Open
University programs (see p. 193) very early and late;
documentaries; travel shows; wildlife programs;
shows about art, history, and classical music; and
hobby-oriented programs about such diverse subjects
as gardening, cookery, chess, and rock music. It even
carries the sheepdog trials ('One man and his dog') in
the early autumn, where you can see the amazing
skills of working sheepdogs.

ITV is operated by different independent companies   *ITV*
in different parts of the country. These companies
produce much of their own programming, but do buy
some from other places. In general, ITV carries
mainstream programs and live sports like the BBC,
but has more soap operas and game shows. It also has
the drawback of showing commercials, although
these are not that frequent and appear mainly
between shows.

Channel 4   Channel 4 was set up as an 'alternative' channel, catering particularly to women and minority interests. It carries some programs of multicultural and feminist interest, foreign films with subtitles, in-depth evening news, current-affairs discussion programs, innovative pop music, and occasionally opera and ballet. It also shows mainstream series, old American series, and films. Channel 4 has commercials too. In Wales, it is the Welsh language channel.

Program times   English TV stations do not broadcast twenty-four hours a day. BBC 1 and ITV begin at 6 a.m. on weekdays. BBC 2 comes on the air at 9 a.m., and Channel 4 doesn't start until late afternoon. Channels usually 'sign off' around midnight on weekdays, and perhaps an hour or so later at weekends – a real live person actually tells you the time, gives you highlights of the next day's viewing, then says 'good night.' Sometimes this is followed by the national anthem.

Programs are scheduled at unpredictable times on the BBC channels, for example at 5:40 or 7:05 (written 7.5). That is, they begin when they need to, since there are no commercials to pad them out. The commercial channels tend to start programs on the half hour. Between shows, the two BBC channels announce what is on each other's station; ITV and Channel 4 have the same arrangement.

Newspapers give daily schedules for all four channels (Sunday schedules are included in the Saturday papers). Local variations in programming are listed at the bottom of the schedule in national papers. In the best tradition of English stubbornness, BBC and ITV prevent anyone from publishing comprehensive weekly TV guides for all four channels. Thus, there are two weekly program guides with misleading titles: the *Radio Times*, which lists BBC TV and radio programs; and *The TV Times*, which gives the commercial stations' programs.

Radio   Radio, or 'the wireless' as it is affectionately called by older English people, is also very good. The station frequencies are listed in the newspapers; note that most stations can be found on both AM and FM. There are four national BBC radio stations (going by the catchy names Radio 1, 2, 3, and 4) which are noncommercial and are financed by the TV license fees. The World Service is intended for listeners outside Britain but can be picked up in southern and eastern parts of the country. The local BBC and commercial radio stations, one or two per locality, tend to be very bland and amateurish. They try to cater to everyone and end up pleasing very few. To fill the need for community and special-interest radio, illegal 'pirate' stations have sprung up. Such stations usually offer only one kind of music or else carry items of interest to a small ethnic or geographical community.

BBC Radio 1 broadcasts from 6 a.m. till midnight and is mainly a Top-40 music channel. It gives the news headlines every hour on the half hour. The disc jockeys on Radio 1 can be extremely irritating – they talk far too much, cut into records just to say something banal, and fill in time with phone-in competitions. One exception is John Peel, who hosts a late-night music program that features up-and-coming groups.

Radio 2 broadcasts on a twenty-four hour basis. Its programs consist mostly of 'easy listening' music and light entertainment, with news summaries on the hour. It also has live sports commentaries.

Radio 3 is on the air from 7 a.m. to 11:30 p.m., playing mainly classical music and a few modern compositions. As well as its various news broadcasts, it offers a smattering of drama, poetry, and jazz.

Radio 4 can be heard from 6 a.m. to midnight. It carries a wide range of non-music programs, many of them excellent. News and weather are given on the hour along with traffic reports. Its varied offerings include discussion and current-affairs programs, plays (often overacted), stories and serialized novels, celebrity quiz shows, comedies, long-running soap operas, and much more. Some of its programs are repeated during the same week.

Newspapers   Britain seems to have the best and the worst newspapers. Fleet Street, as the newspaper industry is called (that's where most major papers used to have their offices), brings out two very different types of paper: the 'quality' papers and the tabloids (also known as the 'gutter press,' not without some justification).

The quality national daily papers contain a good deal of both national and international news in articles of managable length, and include few advertisements. They do not include a page of comic strips. These papers are *The Guardian* (also known as *The Grauniad* because it contains a lot of misprints), which is politically left of center; *The Times*, which gives the Establishment view; and *The Daily Telegraph*, which is to the right of *The Times*. A newcomer is *The Independent*, which aims to fall between *The Guardian* and *The Times*.

In the gutter press, what little news you can find among stories about the Royal Family and TV stars and pictures of scantily-clad women is so trivialized, sensationalized, or biased that it is really not worth reading. The tabloids are *The Daily Mirror*, which is politically left of center; *Today*, a new moderate paper; and *The Daily Mail*, *The Daily Express*, *The Star*, and *The Sun*, which are all right-wing. Interestingly enough, *The Sun* is the best-selling British newspaper.

Sunday papers are independent of daily newspapers of the same title and have different editors. In general, the Sunday papers have far less 'hard' news than the dailies, concentrating on short, readable human-interest stories, travel, and sports. They can also be divided into the quality and tabloid categories. The quality Sundays are *The Observer*, *The Sunday Times*, and *The Sunday Telegraph*. Their price includes a color supplement magazine, which you should be sure to pick up with the paper (the papers and magazines are often in different piles at the newsagent's). The tabloids are *The Mail on Sunday*, *News of the World*, *The Sunday Express*, *The Sunday Mirror*, and *The Sunday People*.

Other national and regional papers of note are *The*

Financial Times, printed on pink paper and aimed at the business community, and *The Morning Star*, the Communist paper. *The Scotsman* and *The Glasgow Herald* are circulated outside Scotland but obviously carry more news about Scotland than the nationals do. There are also local papers in most parts of the country, which combine a little international and national news with items of more local concern.

Some foreign newspapers can be found in central London and in major cities and tourists spots. Most are Continental or U.S. papers, although some from other parts of the world do make an appearance.

Magazines

England does not produce weekly news magazines as such, probably because the daily papers are circulated nationally. However, European editions of *Time* and *Newsweek* are widely available. *The Economist* includes comments on international and national news from a business point of view. Other weekly magazines concentrate mainly on opinion, discussion, and reviews rather than reporting the news; these include *The Spectator* (conservative), *The New Statesman* (socialist), and *New Society* (sociological). *Punch* (weekly) and *Private Eye* (twice monthly) are popular satirical magazines. A large range of special-interest magazines are sold widely in larger newspaper shops such as W H Smith and Menzies.

Crossword puzzles

You may sit down to have a leisurely try at solving a crossword puzzle in a British newspaper or magazine only to find that you haven't got any idea what the peculiar clues are getting at. While papers do have 'normal' crosswords, many also include 'cryptic' crosswords, which can take a long time to get accustomed to. They way the clues work in these is that one or a few words give the meaning of the answer while all the other words are used in various tortuous ways as elements of that answer. You need to know the many conventions and tricks to unravel the clue before you can attempt such crosswords. Certain words signal particular operations: for instance, an anagram (rearrangement of letters) is often signaled by words like *badly*, *develop*, *sort*, *redone*, and words of similar meaning; the words *up*, *back*, *return*, *held up*, etc., usually mean that you have to use a word backward; *one* is often realized as *i* or *a*; and *nothing*, *no*, or *love* become *o* in many cases. Abbreviations also creep into answers: *left* or *learner* becomes *l*; *right* is *r*; *church* is often *CE* (for Church of England); and references to royalty may signal abbreviations like *HRH* (His or Her Royal Highness).

Here are a few examples of clues and their solutions, taken from crosswords in *The Guardian*:

'Nail one left inside not sticking up' = talon. The answer means a kind of *nail* and is formed by putting *a l (one left)* *inside* the word *not*, which has been written backward (*sticking up*).

'Social gathering provides amusement – tonic of sort' = function. The answer means a *social gathering* and is made from *fun (amusement)* and an anagram of *tonic* (signaled by *of sort*).

It helps if you make your first attempt at solving a cryptic crossword with the aid of a competent native. You'll probably find, however, that the challenge makes your brain hurt.

Institutions

The monarchy is one of the oldest and best-loved **Royalty**
institutions in Britain. It may seem surprising that
this relic of an archaic system should survive so
vigorously in this day and age. But in fact, since the
first monarch of a united England, King Athelstan,
came to power in 925, the continuity of royal rule has
been broken only once – when Oliver Cromwell tried
to establish a republic in the 1650s. Such a move
would probably also fail today. Even before this
thousand-year dominance of the royal lineage, Celtic
and Anglo-Saxon kings and queens ruled over regions
of Britain: Queen Boadicea, King Arthur, and King
Alfred the Great are all names well known to the
British.

Various monarchs have given their names to eras
and styles of architecture. Visitors should know the
ones most often referred to, and it will be taken for
granted that you know roughly what dates all these
labels apply to:

Tudor (1485–1605)   Georgian (1714–1830)

Elizabethan (1558–1603)   Victorian (1835–1901)

Jacobean (1605–1620)   Edwardian (1901–1910)

The present monarch is Elizabeth II, By the Grace
of God, Queen of the United Kingdom of Great
Britain and Northern Ireland and Her Other Realms
and Territories, Head of the Commonwealth, Defen-
der of the Faith. Monarchs don't have last names, but
she is of the House of Windsor. Her husband, His
Royal Highness The Prince Philip, is descended from
Greek and other European nobility. He is officially
The Prince Consort, *not* the King. He is usually
referred to as The Duke of Edinburgh, but is also Earl
of Merioneth, Baron of Greenwich, KG, KT, GBE,

PC, and probably has a few other titles. The heir to the throne is HRH Prince Charles Philip Arthur George, Prince of Wales (his most-used title) and Earl of Chester, Duke of Cornwall, Duke of Rothsay, Earl of Carrick, Baron of Renfrew, Lord of the Isles and Great Steward of Scotland, etc., etc., etc. His wife is the very popular Diana, and they have two sons, William and Henry.

Other members of the royal family are: Elizabeth, The Queen Mother (wife of the previous monarch, and Elizabeth II's mother), who loves horse racing and looks just like anyone's granny; Princess Margaret (the Queen's sister), who scandalized the family with her divorce many years ago; Princess Anne, the Queen's daughter, who is a keen horsewoman and is married to Captain Mark Phillips; and the Queen's two youngest sons, Prince Andrew ('randy Andy'), recently wed to Sarah Ferguson, and Prince Edward. An assortment of royal dukes and duchesses and their children completes the main picture.

While the present royal family isn't as aloof from the public as previous ones have been, they do keep a discreet distance, which can be a difficult feat with swarms of tabloid reporters plaguing them wherever they go. It is in their best interests to remain somewhat apart so that the public won't realize that they are just ordinary human beings after all!

The Queen is said to spend much time keeping up with current affairs and is considered to be very well informed on both domestic and foreign matters. Besides her political duties (see below), she and the other Royals have a crowded schedule of public appearances, social occasions, and good causes to attend. Prince Charles and Princess Anne are actively involved in social issues and charities.

The public pays about three-quarters of the royal family's expenses. In 1985, the Civil List (the Royals' allowances) came to £5 million. This money goes on expenses for official duties and for items such as clothes, cars, horses, staff wages, tips, state parties, etc. On top of that £23 million was allotted for the upkeep of the palaces, trains, plane and yachts used by the Royals. The public is allowed minimal access

"Why don't you get off their backs?"

Reproduced by permission of *Punch*

to the royal residences – Kensington Palace, Windsor
Castle (the grounds only), and Sandringham House –
but not Buckingham Palace, unless they are invited to
one of the large garden parties given every summer.
The Queen has to dip into her substantial private
wealth to meet her private expenses.

Some people believe that class divisions in English
society are perpetuated by the very existence of the
monarchy and its accompanying hierarchy of aristocracy. Others are just fed up with having the exploits,
opinions, and everyday movements of the Royals
thrown at them daily and given prominence over
important news items. But then most English people
probably feel that the tradition and uniqueness of this
glamorous anachronism make it definitely worth-
while. The Queen herself is a popular figure.

Nobility   The aristocracy can be seen as a hangover from hundreds of years of royal patronage – the monarchy worked with the support of able men and rewarded them with land and titles. Although the aristocracy was an always-changing group, some families stayed at the top for a very long time, and large tracts of land are still in the possession of a small number of aristocratic families. Others may have only their title left, the wealth having been squandered or heavily taxed. Hardly any new hereditary titles are created by the government today.

The highest-ranking nobles are the dukes and duchesses, some of whom are related to the royal family. Dukes and Duchesses must be addressed by lesser mortals as Your Grace. Next down the hierarchy comes the rank of Marquis and Marchioness, then Earl and Countess. Only women of these higher ranks may be addressed by the title 'Lady.' The lower ranks of the hereditary nobility consist of Viscounts and Viscountesses and Barons and Baronesses. The titles 'Esquire,' 'Gentleman,' and 'Master' (for boys) no longer are reserved for the gentry. It must be said that few English people are interested in, or bothered by, the aristocracy.

Honorary titles are awarded twice a year, on the Queen's (official) birthday and at the New Year. These are given for service to the country, and are awarded to a variety of politicians, industrialists, sportspersons, entertainers, media personalities, artists, etc. The most distinguished honor is a Knighthood – only a knighted man may use the title 'Sir' (his wife becomes a Lady), while a 'knighted' woman goes by the title 'Dame' (but her husband does not get a title). The most common honors are OBE (Officer of the Order of the British Empire) and MBE (Member of the Order of the British Empire), but there are many other honorary awards. Such titles don't carry special privileges.

The title 'Lord of the Manor' means just that: the person owns or is the proprietor of a manor house and its grounds, but isn't necessarily of noble birth.

Britain's government is a constitutional monarchy that operates by means of a parliamentary democracy. That sounds like there's something for everyone – a royal head of state, a constitution, and an elected body representing the common people. However, on closer examination, you find that the Queen has little power, there is no written constitution, and some aspects of the electoral and parliamentary systems are not entirely democratic.

Political system

The Queen is the nominal head of the government, judiciary, armed services, and the Church of England. In fact, she has no real power over them – but she does get in on all the ceremonies. In essence, in her role as head of the government, she has to do what the government of the day wants her to do. Bills that pass through Parliament must be given the 'Royal Assent,' but the days have long since passed when a monarch would refuse to sign a law that the elected bodies had passed.

The monarchy

The only time a monarch can flex her or his political muscle is if there is a 'hung' Parliament – that is, if no party has a majority – or if the majority party has no established leader. Then the monarch can choose the Prime Minister.

Of course, how much influence the Royal Family has is anyone's guess. The Queen is expected not to make public her opinions on governmental matters, although other Royals have recently ignored this convention.

Britain does not have a written constitution or a Bill or Rights: governmental and legal matters are based on common law, drawn from practice and precedence. The government can legislate on anything it wants to, and can undo past laws or even apply new laws retrospectively. An act passed by Parliament cannot be disputed in the law courts. There is also no 'Freedom of Information Act' yet, which has allowed governments to operate with excessive secrecy.

The constitution

Parliament consists of two Houses, one elected and the other not. The House of Commons, the elected

Parliament

body, currently has 650 Members of Parliament, or MPs (of which only twenty-three are women, and none is non-Caucasian). The political party with a majority of seats in the House of Commons forms the government, and that party's leader becomes Prime Minister (PM). The Prime Minister chooses a Cabinet of Ministers from members of her or his party in either House to help in making policy decisions. The opposition party (the largest minority party) forms what is called a 'shadow cabinet,' which is sort of like a government in exile.

MPs are supposed to represent the interests of the people in their constituencies. To keep in touch with their people, MPs hold 'surgeries,' where the constituents come to complain about various matters. When voting in the House, most MPs vote on straight party lines, no matter what that means to the interests of their constituents. To vote against one's party is nearly unforgivable, because if the ruling party loses the vote on a crucial issue, the government can be brought down (if a vote of 'no confidence' is passed), forcing an election. MPs walk into 'yes' or 'no' lobbies when they vote (called a 'division of the House'), so everyone knows who voted which way. If an MP really disagrees with the party line, he or she usually abstains from voting.

Visitors who are eager to see the House in session can apply for entry at their own embassies in London or can line up for admission to the Strangers' Gallery. Parliament is in session from 2:30 p.m. onward Monday through Thursday, and from 9:30 a.m. onward Friday; it is not in session from August to late October. Much of the serious debate goes on in closed committees. However, things can get very lively on Tuesdays and Thursdays during question time, when the Prime Minister or another minister answers questions from the MPs. The purpose of question time isn't really to get answers; it is to score debating points.

The conduct of MPs can be quite surprising. They laugh at, jeer at, and heckle each other, and even try to shout down speakers. Cries of 'Rubbish!' or 'Hear, hear' fill the background. Broadcasts of proceedings (on Radio 4 at 8:40 a.m.) often sound like they are coming from a classroom full of unruly schoolboys. During all this, though, some outward appearance of civility is maintained. MPs must refer to each other as 'The Honorable Gentleman' or 'The Right Honorable Member,' and will say that someone is not being entirely candid or is not well informed when they really mean to say he is an ignorant liar. Verbal abuse, if not withdrawn formally, is punished by the offending MP being 'named' and suspended for a few days.

Elections Elections for Parliament must be held every five years, but can be held sooner if the government thinks it is advantageous. Any resident of the Commonwealth and any Irish citizen who lives in Britain can vote if registered and over eighteen. Mercifully, election campaigns are limited to about three weeks, with limits also placed on the amount of campaign money spent and the number of TV and radio 'party political broadcasts.' In each election area, whichever candidate gets the most votes wins the seat in Parliament. There is no requirement that this has to be over 50 percent of the votes cast, and there is no system of proportional representation.

Political parties Until recently, there had been only two major political parties in Britain: the Conservatives (called Tories), which is politically to the right, and Labour, to the left. The Liberals, long a minority center party, have recently formed an alliance with the new Social Democratic Party, also near the center of the political spectrum. There are many fringe parties, including the Ecology Party, the Socialist Workers' Party (Marxists), the National Front (racists), the Scottish Nationalists, Plaid Cymru (Welsh nationalists); and a variety of 'lunatic fringe' parties, such as the League of Empire Loyalists, Death off Roads – Freight on Rail Party, the Official Monster Raving Loony Party, and others. Northern Ireland has seventeen seats in Parliament; its main parties are the Official Unionists (Protestants); the Democratic Unionists (Protestant extremists); the Social Democratic and Labour Party

(Catholics); and the Provisional Sinn Fein (Catholic extremists).

House of Lords

There are now more than a thousand *Peers* who are entitled to sit in the House of Lords. None of these people is elected. Life Peers are those appointed by the government as a form of political patronage. They may attend the House of Lords until they die, but cannot pass on their privilege. Hereditary Peers, on the other hand, are there because some forefather was a noble, and the privilege is passed on through the generations. Most Hereditary Peers do not regularly attend the House of Lords (some have renounced their titles). The Lords Spiritual are the bishops and archbishops of the Church of England. There are also a few Law Lords, who function as the highest court of appeal, headed by the Lord Chancellor. The Lord Chancellor is also speaker of the House of Lords and presides from the *woolsack* (a medieval seat stuffed with wool from Commonwealth countries).

The House of Lords normally has a low attendance (between 30 and 300). Members don't get a salary, but can claim expenses when attending a session. Their main function is to revise and amend bills that have come from the House of Commons. The Lords can't legislate on their own, but they do have to pass bills that have gone through the Commons. It is rare for them actually to defeat a bill, but they can make amendments and express disapproval by delaying a non-finance bill by up to a year.

There has been some talk about abolishing the House of Lords and perhaps replacing it with a second elected body. Of course, the Lords would have to vote for their own abolition before that could take place!

Local government

Local government is organized both by county and by town. One important function of local government is to set the local *rates* (property taxes) at a level high enough to provide for the local services it feels are important, which means that some areas have better public services than others. However, this power is about to be interfered with by the national government, which has, in fact, already succeeded in abolishing the large metropolitan elected councils that coordinate services over large urban areas.

A *city* can call itself a city only if it has been granted a royal charter. Every city has a ceremonial Lord Mayor, who appears at official functions and wears a large chain and cloak. The post is appointed each year in recognition of service to the area.

Law and order

The English bobby (policeman) has a wonderful image abroad, although British blacks and strikers aren't so enamored of them. Most visitors find bobbies to be courteous, helpful, nonthreatening, and, of couse, quaint. Many bobbies still do their rounds on foot or on a bicycle, while others patrol in 'panda' cars. The police are mainly unarmed; they carry hard truncheons (batons), but are issued guns only in exceptional circumstances.

New Scotland Yard (or The Yard) of detective-novel fame, which is the headquarters for the Metropolitan Police, is located not in Scotland but in London. The security and espionage organizations of James Bond fame (known as MI5 and MI6) do not officially exist. They are also located in London.

Lawyers

The legal profession consists of *solicitors* and *barristers*. Solicitors perform the normal duties of most lawyers in other countries; however, although they prepare cases for court, they are not allowed to argue certain classes of cases before judge and jury. This responsibility falls to a barrister, who might not even have direct contact with the client. (Of course, the client pays for the services of both professionals.) Judges are drawn exclusively from the ranks of barristers; they both wear long black robes and curly white wigs.

Notaries

A Commissioner of Oaths is the person you go to when you need a notarized signature.

Religion

The Church of England, also known as the Anglican Church, is the official state religious denomination. The ruling monarch must belong to the Church of

England and is its nominal head. The Church of England has been called the 'Tory Party at prayer' because of its conservativism, but some clergy take fairly radical stands on social and religious issues.

The C of E operates in the 'high church' tradition, with a lot of ritual, fine trappings, and hierarchical organization. It tolerates a wide variety of doctrinal interpretations, but women are still not allowed to become vicars (clergy). Nor are girls or women allowed to sing in the impressive choirs of the grand cathedrals – instead, little boys dressed in robes sing the high parts.

Although (or because) religious instruction is compulsory in schools, few people actually attend church regularly (the current estimate is about 10 percent of the population). Congregations do swell at Easter and Christmas. Be warned – some of the older churches are very cold in winter, and these are very unlikely to have toilets. In rural areas, several country churches may share a vicar on a monthly rotation.

Many other religions are well represented in England. Since the Irish form the largest minority in England, there are many Catholic churches around. Catholics often have newer churches and cathedrals, for most of the medieval churches, originally Catholic, later became Anglican. Quaker, Methodist, and United Reform (Congregational and Presbyterian) churches can be found in many towns, along with smaller Christian denominations. There are Jews, Moslems, Sikhs, and Hindus scattered throughout the country, often in the larger cities. Kosher foods are available in London, and Hallal meats in most large cities.

As in most other aspects of their private lives, the English tend to be quiet about their personal religious beliefs. Some evangelism is creeping in from the U.S., but it is still in a minority. Religious programs on TV and radio are mainly confined to Sundays, short morning services (daily on Radio 4 at 10:30) and a 'thought for the day' (just before the 8 a.m. news on Radio 4).

To find out about church services and functions, ask at a Tourist Information Centre or look in local newspapers. Most churches advertise service times on a notice board outside.

The education system in England is generally quite good, although recently there has been much concern over slipping standards, perhaps due in part to large cuts in funding for education. There is still a split between state-run (the large majority) and private education.

The school year begins in September and runs until mid-July. Schools 'break up' at the end of each of three terms, with 10 to 14 days' holiday after the first two and six weeks off in the summer. There are also half-term holidays of one week or so in the middle of each term, to let both teachers and students regain their sanity. Most schools try to organize trips during some of the holidays, with younger students going to other parts of Britain and older ones usually going abroad. The school day usually starts at 9 a.m. and goes until 3:30 or 4 p.m.

All state-run schools are free of charge. There are very few state-aided nursery schools, however, so many working parents must pay for private preschool groups. Primary education starts with *infant school* for the five- to seven- year-olds (the term seems somewhat insulting). This is followed by *junior* or *first school* for children from the ages of seven through eleven. In some areas junior school ends at the age of nine and is followed by *middle school*.

In the old education system, students took an exam at the age of eleven called the *11 plus*. The results of this exam determined whether or not the student could go on to a *grammar school* (for the top students) or had to go to a *secondary modern school* (for those who didn't pass). Semi-selective *direct grant schools* also existed, taking students who passed the 11 plus for free, but also taking in students of lesser ability who could pay for the privilege. This two-track system has been abandoned in most places, and the 11 plus exam has been scrapped. Secondary schools are now usually totally *comprehensive* (non-selective); but a few grammar schools still exist.

Comprehensives are divided into six *forms*, or years, with the first form having the youngest children. At the age of sixteen (the end of the fifth form), students can take either CSE (Certificate of Secondary Education) or O-level (Ordinary) exams; or they just leave school. A new set of exams, called GCSE, is now replacing the CSE and O levels. Students can then stay on for the sixth form and spend two or three years specializing in three subjects. (About 20 to 30 percent of students do stay on.) At the end of sixth form, the students take their A-level (Advanced) exams, which determine whether or not they get a place at a university. Sixth-form students have a lot of non-instructional time at school to 'revise' (prepare) for these exams. Some areas have special sixth-form colleges, which are separate from the rest of the secondary comprehensives.

In general, there is little testing or grading in most schools, compared to that in the education systems in many other countries. Primary schools in particular are lively and easygoing. At all levels, students are provided with bound notebooks to do their work in, and these progressive records are assessed and commented on. (A 'tick' (check mark) means an answer is correct, while an *x* means it is wrong.) Written reports about the students are sent home at various times of the year.

Headmasters and headmistresses (also called head teachers or just heads) are in charge of the schools and have a great deal of say in the school's policy. Thus there is quite a bit of variation in what is taught and how it is taught, depending upon the school and the region of the country. Many schools are putting more emphasis on muticultural education and vocational subjects now, while others are concentrating on the traditional subjects. The only subject that a school is required by law to teach is religion. The school day has to start with an act of collective worship as well, although some schools have replaced the Church of England bias with comparative religion or issues of morality.

Activities such as choir or orchestra and some sports take place after school, or traditionally on

Wednesday afternoons.

Physical punishment is rare, though some schools still make use of the cane on hands or backsides.

Confusingly enough, the larger and more famous private fee-paying boarding schools, such as Eton, Harrow, Rugby, and Roedean, are called 'Public Schools.' They were originally founded by charitable benefactors for families who valued an education but who couldn't afford private tutors. When free state-run schooling came along, these fee-paying schools retained the title 'public schools', but became institutions mainly for the rich.

Private schools

Public Schools (which now prefer to be called Independent schools) mainly educate students who are between the ages of twelve and eighteen, but there

Reproduced from *Scene Changes* by Osbert Lancaster by permission of John Murray

are private 'preparatory' primary schools that feed into the system. Public Schools are usually boarding schools, and thus are often also single-sex institutions. These bastions of tradition often occupy buildings steeped in tradition and history. Traditional values, including a high regard for authority and self-discipline, are stressed in many. Some are run by religious establishments, some by private groups.

The purpose of education at private schools used to be to turn out gentlemen and ladies. Nowadays, private schools strive to give their students a solid academic education (which is not necessarily better than that from a state-run school) as well as build confidence and 'character' (often through getting knocked about on a rugby pitch). The students also benefit from acquiring the 'right' accent (see p. 83) and good connections that will help them after they have left school (the 'old boy network'). Indeed, it seems that if you want to do well in government, the foreign service, or the higher echelons of business, it helps to have gone to a good private school.

Uniforms Most schools, both private and state-run, require pupils to wear school uniforms or a restricted range of colors and styles of clothing. It seems that the more exclusive the school, the more ridiculous the uniform. Most school uniforms consist of a blazer or sweater and a tie (for both boys and girls), and trousers or skirts and dresses of a particular color and type. Shirts and socks must match the uniform. Eton, probably the most exclusive Public School, makes its pupils wear morning suits (tailcoats and top hats)!

Small boys often aren't allowed to wear long trousers until they are eleven or twelve (they wear out the knees too quickly). In winter a common sight is little boys wearing ties, caps, shorts, and long socks, and sporting very red, or even blue, knees. Even during sports time, boys are girls bare their legs to the elements.

Higher education Britain has forty-seven state-run but autonomous universities and almost as many polytechnics; there is one private university. University and polytechnic degree programs last for three or four years, while those at colleges of higher education provide one- or two-year non-degree courses. Only about 5 percent of 'school leavers' go on to university. Every British undergraduate university student has all higher educational fees generously paid for by the government and receives a means-tested grant (stipend) to pay for living expenses. Undergraduate students from the EEC pay reduced fees; foreign students from outside the EEC and students working on graduate degrees must pay all fees themselves.

Terms

The university year runs from the beginning of October to the beginning of July. Terms are about ten weeks long, with four or five weeks off around Christmas and Easter.

Rooms

Rooms in a hall of residence (dormitory) are usually single occupancy. They tend to be a bit small, but most do have a washbasin in the room. So that students don't have to interrupt their thoughts too much with domestic matters, rooms are cleaned and sometimes even beds made by the cleaning staff at many universities. Most residence halls provide a bar and a games room.

Courses

The British university system is quite different from that in many other countries. Students are admitted to study a particular subject or combination of subjects – such as French and linguistics, or economics and politics – and those may be the only subjects they study for the entire time. The assumption is that they will already have had a well-rounded education at secondary school and will know exactly what they want to study. If a student's interests change, it may be difficult to switch from one subject to another.

Classes may meet only once a week. Lectures are supplemented with small group tutorials or seminars, during which the instructor goes over material connected with the lecture and assigns essays and further reading. This type of schedule leaves much free time for students to read widely and spend time thinking, if they are disciplined enough to make good use of the time. Work is often assigned over holiday periods.

Degrees   There is little in the way of continual assessment on many courses, so a great deal depends on the comprehensive exams students take at the end of their three or four years. This puts a lot of pressure on them. They often have to 'sit' as many as ten three-hour exams. Someone from another university also grades the exams, and students may have to give an oral defense of their exam answers (called a *viva*) in front of the internal and external examiners. Bachelor's degrees are ranked by their 'class' number, which signals how well the student did. The highest distinction (and a rare one) is a first-class degree. A 2.1 is very good, a 2.2 is average, and a third-class degree is poor. A 'pass' degree is given in recognition of having wasted three years at university. Few students fail outright, because if they are doing that badly, they usually aren't allowed to get as far as taking their exams. In general, an English Bachelor's degree is on a par with an American Master's degree. Scottish universities award a Master's degree for completing an undergraduate program.

What the English call Master's degree programs are usually one-year courses in a subject other than the student's undergraduate one. Students who want to do post-graduate work in the same subject area as their undergraduate work usually sign up for either a two-year M.Phil. (Master of Philosophy) or a three-year Ph.D. research program.

Staff   Most university departments have only one person titled Professor (who is rarely the eccentric gray-haired, pipe-smoking bachelor in a tweed jacket portrayed in films). The next step down the faculty hierarchy is Reader (a person who teaches as well as reads); then comes Senior Lecturer, with Lecturer at the bottom. The administrative head of the university is the Vice-Chancellor (the Chancellorship is an honorary post).

Students don't go out of their way to show that they
belong to a particular university. Some may wear
scarves that incorporate the university's colors, but
few would wear a T-shirt with the university name on
it. No one goes to watch university sports teams
except close friends of the players. *School spirit*

Oxford and Cambridge universities are by far the
most prestigious to attend and are the oldest and most
traditional of universities as well. Royalty and the
intelligent aristocracy receive their education at these
institutions, and half the students come from private
schools. Some of the 'Oxbridge' colleges still require
students to sit special entrance exams. The division
into colleges at Oxford and Cambridge is for residential and tutorial, not academic, purposes. Their university terms last only eight weeks, which gives these
students more free time to think their great thoughts. *Oxbridge*

Some of the 'dons' (lecturers) at Oxford and
Cambridge still wear their academic gowns when
lecturing and dining in the hall. (At one time students
too had to wear them in class, at dinner, and on the
streets at night.) At dinners on special occasions the
academics, in their gowns, proceed into the hall and
up to the 'high table,' which is usually on a platform
so they can look down on the students. Someone says
grace, probably in Latin, and then waiters serve up a
five-course meal, complete with wine. Afterward, the
academics recess to have port and smoke cigars. It's
all very pompous.

The Open University offers part-time higher education for those who work or who can't afford the time
or disruption of going back to university. It is a type
of correspondence education system, including lectures given over the radio or TV at very unsocial
hours. Students write essays, meet with tutors occasionally, and attend sessions in the summer for a few
weeks. It usually takes six or seven years to get a
degree this way. The quality of work demanded for
an Open University degree is high, and the fees are
very moderate. *The Open University*

The welfare state Britain was a pioneer in the concept of the welfare state. In theory, everyone is supposed to be looked after adequately 'from cradle to grave.' In fact, this doesn't always happen, as recent cuts in government funding have reduced many state benefits. Benefits include such things as free medical care, child allowances (a weekly amount given to parents, per child), mobility allowances for the handicapped, domestic help for the elderly, unemployment benefit, supplementary benefit and rent rebates for the low-paid, old-age pensions, maternity grants, and death (funeral) grants.

About one-third of the housing in England is council housing, which is built and maintained by the local governments. Some of this public housing is very nice indeed, and consists of both houses with gardens and flats. However, the government is now selling off its public housing at very cheap prices and is not building many new council houses or repairing the crumbling older ones. There are long waiting lists of people who want to live in council houses because they can't afford to buy their own house or rent privately. Some people have been housed temporarily in hotels and bed-and-breakfast places, sometimes for well over a year, at great public expense.

NHS One of the prides of the British welfare system is the National Health Service (NHS), which was set up in 1946 to ensure that everyone had equal access to good medical care. Originally, all medical attention was free, with funds for the service coming from taxes. As the cost of medicines and equipment has risen, some charges have been passed on to the patients. While all hospital treatment, ambulance service, and checkups by doctors, dentists, and ophthalmologists are still free (except for an emergency treatment charge of about £14 for drivers involved in road accidents), people now pay set charges for prescriptions, dental work, and glasses, which are usually far below the actual costs. GPs (general practitioners) still make free house calls, and community health workers and district nurses visit people at home who are convalescent, bed ridden, or who have new babies to make sure they are getting on all right.

Private medicine exists alongside the NHS and is now being encouraged, to save the government a lot of money. Most private patients are treated in NHS hospitals by state-trained doctors who earn extra money through taking private patients. People are tempted to go for private treatment in order to get around the long queues for minor operations, but most people do not yet have private medical insurance to help pay the costs. Alternative forms of medicine such as osteopathy, acupuncture, etc., are not recognized by the NHS and so must be paid for by the individual. Foreigners who come to Britain for special medical treatment are considered private patients and must pay the costs.

If you are a legal resident in England and want to join the NHS, you should register with a particular GP and go to him or her whenever you need to. You can change doctors if you are not satisfied with yours, as long as another doctor has room on his or her list. If you need to see a specialist, you must go first to your GP, who will refer you to the specialist for free treatment (without a referral, you will have to pay). Visitors to England who need to see a doctor should just phone or visit the nearest one. You will have to pay.

English doctors tend not to explain things to patients in detail unless asked, which can be infuriating if you don't know the right questions.

The quality of care by the medical profession is good, but financial pressures on the system have led to recent cutbacks in staff and facilities at hospitals and clinics. There are long waiting lists for many types of non-emergency operations. In general, the NHS is very good for emergency care, but not so wonderful for chronic non-emergency or preventive care. However, more preventive advice and screening are becoming available.

English characteristics and attitudes

It is impossible (and unfair) to categorize a nation of individuals, for there are far too many exceptions to any generalization. The English are, however, associated with certain characteristics and attitudes with some justification. To really know the people, though, it's best to become familiar enough with them to be able to move beyond the stereotypes. This can be somewhat difficult since, although they may have strong feelings, they tend not to be very demonstrative.

Restraint The English have a reputation for being unflappable – cool, calm, and collected – in the face of both failure and success, anger and joy. It is 'not the done thing' to make any kind of scene. They tend to talk softly (except for a certain type of upper-class person), and do not often show emotion or affection openly. They are certainly not rude in public – it is important to keep up the appearance of civility at all times. Politeness and quiet dignity are supposed to be the norm. Exceptions can always be found – especially late on Saturday nights!

The sense of restraint means containing one's enthusiasm to a large degree. It is not seemly for adults to be too 'keen' about anything; showing too much enthusiasm is slightly suspect. The English may be committed to a cause and even campaign for something, but they don't get worked up into a frenzy over it.

It is also very bad form to boast about oneself or one's family or to be too ambitious, especially about money. Even in situations like job interviews, people who try to sell themselves too hard are suspected of being arrogant and pushy; modesty is a highly valued trait. The English also don't compliment other people readily, nor do they know how to react to a compliment.

To get around showing much enthusiasm, the English have perfected the art of understatement. If they *really* like something, they will say it is 'very good, indeed,' and leave it at that. If they have done well, then they are 'quite pleased' with their efforts. Someone who has just performed an act of amazing skill or bravery gets a 'well done' or 'jolly good show.' People who go in for overstatement are thought to be insincere or patronizing.

The English are generally not ostentatious about their possessions, either. Flaunting wealth is definitely tacky. They certainly aren't flashy dressers: women tend to wear practical (but tasteful) rather than highly fashionable clothing; and men who bother about how they look often dress in conservative, sedate clothes. They tend to be frugal in a variety of ways – lavish spending on luxury items, serving huge portions of food, and bathing more than once or twice a week are seen by some as extravagant vices.

Their restraint may make the English seem apathetic or complacent, but this is sometimes just because they are timid. If something goes wrong they remark 'mustn't grumble,' and make the best of it. They don't complain to the right people when they've had bad service, faulty goods, or poorly prepared food – they just moan about it to themselves. If they do work up the courage to complain, they often apologize for doing so. They generally hate to draw attention to themselves in public.

The younger generation, however, has tried to distance itself from all this moderation. Some younger people sport brightly colored spiked hair (or shaved heads), strange clothing combinations, and engage in flamboyant behaviour, intended to show that they are much less inhibited than their parents.

Hospitality

The English don't make a fuss over strangers or friends. When meeting a stranger in a business or formal situation, men shake hands, as do some younger women. They tend not to shake hands on parting, however, nor on subsequent meetings. Close friends may exchange a quick kiss on the cheek when meeting or parting, but there is rarely any kissing or embracing between men.

The southern English in particular are known for not being overly hospitable to strangers and neighbors. Some visitors therefore think them cold and reserved, but they are actually quite friendly and helpful in a quiet sort of way. If they seem reluctant to commit themselves to further encounters with you, this is not snobbishness, but really a way of avoiding embarrassment in case they don't like you or you don't like them. They'd rather play it safe. It takes time to make friends with English people, and you can't rush the process. Once you do strike up a friendship with an English person, though, you can usually be sure that it is sincere, and will last.

Privacy   The English value privacy quite strongly. The phrase 'he keeps himself to himself' is a mark of approval. Just as they enclose their gardens to keep out prying eyes, they hide away their private lives and feelings. They don't readily reveal personal details to friends, let alone to strangers, nor do they ask for them from others. In fact, you can have a long conversation with an English person and not know his or her name at the end of it. It can also be difficult at times to draw out someone's personal beliefs and opinions. This reticence may be due to a general lack of confidence, a fear of boring people or a reluctance to confide in someone who may be only a passing acquaintance, but more often it's just that they don't think it's anyone else's business.

One place where you can see uncharacteristic displays of unrestrained, public opinions is at Speaker's Corner in Hyde Park in London. On Sundays, assorted crusaders and oddballs stand up and air their views to whoever will listen.

The English don't tend to be gregarious and are not great joiners of large clubs, preferring to pursue their interests individually. They also shy away from getting involved in other people's affairs or jumping in to help sort out a public disturbance – it is not their business, as far as they are concerned, and could be embarrassing.

Perhaps because of their restraint and respect for privacy, the English are very tolerant of people who are a little eccentric, as long as they are harmless and quiet. No one complains or even comments much if a neighbor keeps twenty cats in a small cottage, or fills a house with carnivorous plants, or makes scale models of cathedrals from matchsticks. It is that person's right and privilege to do whatever he or she wants to do, so long as it isn't a nuisance to others.

The English value effort and fair play, and tend to sympathise with the 'underdog' in any situation. The English sporting motto has long been 'it's not whether you win or lose, it's how you play the game.' This extends to all facets of life, where it is essentially the *trying* that counts. Heroic failures – such as Scott's fatal attempt to reach the South Pole (he took *ponies* with him to pull the sleds), or the disastrous Charge of the Light Brigade during the Crimean War – are celebrated as if they were victories: at least they all tried.

Amateurness

However, those who appear to be too single-minded and ambitious may be regarded with suspicion.

The English are very endearing in the way they trust other people. If you say you have certain qualifications, they believe you and often don't ask you to supply proof of this. For some business people, your word or handshake is still enough to seal a deal.

Interwoven with all this is shortsightedness. The English tend to paper over the cracks because they didn't take steps to prevent them in the first place. Problems like pollution, aging infrastructures, and enforcing safety standards aren't tackled until it is too late in many cases, even if there has been adequate forewarning. Sometimes this is due to cuts in funding, but that in itself shows a certain myopia. Rather than putting their minds towards doing something efficiently, they often just 'muddle through.'

This isn't to say that the British aren't clever. They have provided the world with many important inventions and ideas. But sadly they don't seem able to make the most of their creativity – they leave it to some foreign entrepreneur to exploit their ideas.

Bloody-mindedness

One of the less endearing character traits of the English is bloody-mindedness – stubborn, awkward, or uncooperative behavior. This is fairly common in so-called service encounters, although there have been attempts to improve the quality of service in some spheres. Bloody-mindedness does not necessarily involve rudeness; people .can refuse to be cooperative and still have a smile on their face. Those who are unpleasant as well as stubborn, are said to be *stroppy* (obstreperous); someone who is uncooperative and short-tempered is said to be *shirty*; and someone who disagrees a lot is *bolshy*.

The English tend to be stubborn about individual principles rather than about ideologies as a whole. Most problems in industrial relations seem like exercises in bloody-mindedness.

Humor

The English have a dry sense of humor. Indeed, irony, understatement, sarcasm, and puns are the mainstays of their jokes and witty remarks. It can be very difficult for outsiders to tell whether or not an English person is being funny or serious, so don't take quick offense at some remark aimed at you - it could easily be meant in jest. Cockneys (working-class Londoners) and Liverpudlians are well known for their quick wit and repartee.

English humor also extends to the outrageously ridiculous. What other country could have given the world Monty Python?!

Sexuality

The English are not known for being red-hot lovers or sex symbols. Perhaps that is because they're private and reserved about personal matters. As a song by Eartha Kitt comparing the courtship behavior of men goes, 'an Englishman takes time'. Teenagers don't usually have their own cars, so they must go on dates by bicycle, bus, or with a gang of friends in someone's parents' car, none of which allows for much intimacy or a romantic atmosphere. Nevertheless the English can be sentimental and romantic.

British men in general don't make a big thing out of being macho – indeed many still pride themselves on being gallant and chivalrous. Many foreigners suspect

English males of being slightly effeminate, especially the more upper-class men, but their little affectations are just cultural and don't mean that they are homosexuals (or 'poofs'). Homosexuality is fairly well tolerated anyway, as long as it remains a private practice.

English women have a reputation for being passive. There's a well-known myth that mothers used to advise their daughters to 'lie back and think of England'. However, while this myth may have held some truth in the Victorian times from which it stems, it no longer reflects the attitudes of recent generations of women who have fought for the right to take initiatives and make decisions in all areas of life.

Attitudes toward animals

The English love animals and often have a lot of pets. They look after them very well, without being too silly about them (you won't find commercial dog-cemeteries in England!). Dogs, cats, and budgies (budgerigars, a kind of parakeet) are the most common pets.

There are many wild animal refuges for injured, orphaned, or endangered animals and birds, which are often run by volunteers. In general, the English public has respect for both wild and domestic animals.

Social class

England has a very class-conscious society. Although some class barriers have been breaking down, people still notice all those little clues to a person's social origins. It's breeding, not money, that talks. Accents give away both regional and social information, as do schools attended, houses, furniture styles etc.

Besides normal clues to status, leisure activities can also indicate social class (see Sport and recreation). Clothing can signal class (not just in the obvious sense that richer people have better and newer clothes): for example, men wearing flat-billed cloth caps are usually working-class, while men wearing any other kind of hat are likely to be upper-middle or upper class; and women wearing thick tweed coats, head scarves, and green Wellington boots are often upper-class gentry. Names can be telling – anyone named Tristram or Fiona is definitely upper-middle or upper class, while Lee or Tracey would be lower. Double-barrelled surnames (like Gordon-Jones) also imply upper-classness. To some extent class variety takes the place of the ethnic or simple wealth-related distinctions of other societies.

Women   Attitudes to women differ according to social class. Both upper and lower class men try to distance themselves from their women: upper-class men attend single-sex private schools and join gentlemen's clubs for their entertainment; lower-class men go to working men's clubs or to sports events with their male 'mates'. Middle-class women get away from their men by joining charitable organizations and clubs.

Even though Britain is headed by both a female Prime Minister and the Queen, women remain second-class citizens in many respects. They rarely make it to the top of their professions; many men just don't like working for women, and free subsidized day nurseries aren't readily available for working mothers (nannies are quite expensive). Even though there has been legislation outlawing sexual discrimination in employment, women aren't as well paid as men because they tend to be concentrated in the lower-status jobs. They often don't get help with the housework from their men even if they work full-time. However, slow progress towards equal opportunities for women is being made as women become increasingly ambitious and ever more determined to win the fight against discrimination.

Attitudes to   There is a tongue-in-cheek song that goes 'The
foreigners   British, the British, the British are best, I wouldn't give tuppence for none of the rest.' A surprising number of the natives seem to actually feel this way. Some still pine for the golden days of the British Empire, when Britannia ruled the waves, Britain was 'top nation,' and all the foreigners knew their place.

In many communities, ethnic groups and natives live alongside one another peacefully, but some of the

English still refuse to accept that other cultures have valuable or interesting things to contribute, and racism is a well-recognized problem, particularly in inner-city poor areas. Immigrants and their children from many of the 'new colonies' – especially the Indian subcontinent and the West Indies – suffer racial abuse and attacks from a small but vocal section of society.

The English do not usually think of themselves as Europeans. About the only time they are happy to be classed with the Europeans is when trying to distance themselves from American policies!

The English have respect for the accomplishments of America, France, Germany, and Japan, but they also consider Americans to be naïve, loud, pushy, and insincere, the French arrogant and dogmatic, the Germans humorless and punctilious, and the Japanese too deferential and too eager to work hard. They find Australians a bit brash and unsophisticated, the Mediterranean peoples emotional and disorganized, and Arabs ostentatious and backward. They don't particularly like the Soviets, but at least they aren't paranoid about them.

The British also hold stereotypes about themselves, of course. They distinguish themselves, the 'calm' Anglo-Saxons, from those 'excitable' Celts (the Scots, Welsh, and Irish). The Celts, of course, have equally unflattering things to say about the English, who they consider to be cold, arrogant, patronizing, and self-centered. The English also divide themselves into northerners and southerners: stereotypical northerners are supposed to be friendly, unsophisticated, chauvinistic, heavy drinkers, while southerners are stuffy, effete, cold, and ambitious. Rural folk anywhere in the country are known for not talking much.

Don't worry about meeting up with snobbish, inhibited, or bloody-minded English people – deep down, they are really jolly decent chaps. You'll find that they're generally helpful and friendly if you approach them the same way, and when you've made friends with the English you'll probably stay friends. And the tens of thousands of tourists, foreign students, and businesspeople who come to this country can attest to the fact that England really isn't difficult to cope with. Things may be different from what you're used to, but that is part of the attraction of traveling to a new country and experiencing another culture. On the whole, you will find the English gracious and helpful, the country beautiful and fascinating, and the weather ... well ... very English.

Conversion Tables for Weights and Measures

length
1 mile = 1.61 kilometers
1 yard = 0.91 meters
1 inch = 2.54 centimeters

volume
1 Imperial pint (20 fluid ounces) = 1.2 U.S. pint = 0.57 litre
1 Imperial gallon = 1.2 U.S. gallon = 4.55 litres

weight
1 ounce = 28.35 grams
1 pound (16 ounces) = 0.45 kilograms
1 stone = 14 pounds

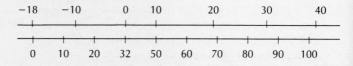

Celsius	−18	−10	0	10	20	30	40
Fahrenheit	0	10	20	32	50	60	70	80	90	100

cooking   oven temperature

Fahrenheit	Celsius	Gas mark
300	150	2
325	160	3
350	180	4
375	190	5
400	200	6

1 ounce = approximately 2 tablespoons

Note that British tablespoons are a little larger than U.S. ones and slightly smaller than Australian ones.

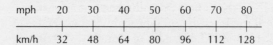

speeds

mph	20	30	40	50	60	70	80
km/h	32	48	64	80	96	112	128

Appendix: Useful Addresses

British Tourist Authority, Thames Tower, **Tourist**
  Black's Road, Hammersmith, London W6 9EL **offices**
  Telephone: 01–846 9000
English Tourist Board, Thames Tower, Black's Road,
  Hammersmith, London W6 9EL
  Telephone: 01–846 9000
London Tourist Board (National Tourist
  Information Centre, Victoria Station Forecourt),
  26 Grosvenor Gardens, London SW1W 0ET
  Telephone: 01–730 3488

British Travel Centre, 12 Regent Street, Piccadilly **Travel**
  Circus, London
  Telephone: 01–730 3400
Thomas Cook, 45 Berkeley Square, London W1
  Telephone: 01–499 4000

Automobile Association (AA), Fanum House, **Driving**
  5 New Coventry Street, London W1V 8HT
  Telephone: 01–839 4355
Royal Automobile Club (RAC), PO Box 100,
  RAC House, Landsdowne Road, East Croydon,
  London CR9 2JA
  Telephone: 01–686 2525

British Hotels, Restaurants and Caterers Association, **Accommoda-**
  40 Duke Street, London W1 **tion**
  Telephone: 01–499 6641
Youth Hostels Association, Trevelyan House,
  8 St. Stephens Hill, St. Albans, Herts AL1 2DY
  Telephone: (0727) 55215 (0727) 55218

American Express, 32 Grosvenor Square, **Banking**
  London W1
  Telephone: 01–409 0838

Embassies   Australian High Commission, Australia House,
                 The Strand, London WC2
                 Telephone: 01–438 8000
                 Canadian High Commission, Canada House,
                 Trafalgar Square, London SW1
                 Telephone: 01–629 9492
                 French Embassy, 21 Grosvenor Place, London SW1
                 Telephone: 01–235 5148
                 German Federal Republic Embassy,
                 23 Belgrave Square, London SW1
                 Telephone: 01–235 5033
                 Japanese Embassy, 21 Grosvenor Place, London W1
                 Telephone: 01–493 6030
                 US Embassy, 24 Grosvenor Square, London W1A
                 Telephone: 01–499 9000

British   Australia: 4th Floor, Midland House,
Tourist   171 Clarence Street, Sydney NSW 2000
Authority   Telephone: 010 61 2 29 8627
overseas   Canada: 94 Cumberland Street, Suite 600, Toronto,
offices   Ontario M5R 3N3
                 Telephone: 010 1416 961 8124
                 France: 63 Rue Pierre-Charron, 75008 Paris
                 Telephone: 010 33 1 42 89 01 77
                 Germany and Austria: Neue Mainzer Strasse 22 6000,
                 Frankfurt 1
                 Telephone: 010 49 69 23 807 44
                 Japan: 246 Tokyo Club Building,
                 3–2–6 Kasumigaseki, Chiyoda-Ku, Tokyo 100
                 Telephone: 01081 3 581 5797
                 USA: 3rd Floor 40 West 57th Street New York
                 NY 10019
                 Telephone: 010 1 212 581 4700

Index

Topics are indexed under their American name, followed by the English equivalent in brackets; for example, 'drapes (curtains)'.

Index by Meg Davies

Suggestions

This page can be used to send in your suggestions for improving the book. What vital matters have been overlooked? What difficulties and pitfalls have been neglected or glossed over? What else should the intending visitor know about the quirks of the English way of life? Please write and tell us.

If your suggestions are adopted in the revised edition, you will receive a free copy in recognition of your services in helping other people cope with England.

Please send your suggestions to Jean Hannah,
c/o Basil Blackwell Ltd.,
108 Cowley Road, Oxford OX4 1JF.

Name ....

Address ....

....

My suggestions are